Shakti Farts

& Belly Laughs

What really happens when wild women gather

A collaborative book project from The Unbound Press

ISBN:
978-1-913590-48-2 (Paperback)
978-1-913590-49-9 (ebook)

Cover design by Lynda Mangoro.
Cover artwork by Zoe Foster. Close-up detail from "Goddess Rising" by Zoë K. M. Foster, ©2021 zoekmfoster.com

The Unbound Press
www.theunboundpress.com

I couldn't stand being in that room. I had to get out.

The lunch break was my escape. I made sure I was one of the first out of the room. (Goddess forbid that anyone would ask me whether I wanted to join them). I walked out into the busy, pre-Christmas crowds, determined not to return.

London. December 2016.

I was at Rebecca Campbell's 'Rise Sister Rise' event. And I was deeply uncomfortable. You know that feeling when you can't stand being in your own skin? I hated the feeling of my body against the seat. I couldn't sit still. The energy felt oppressive.

Why was I feeling like this?

Logically it didn't make sense. The women gathered in the room were obviously amazing. Rebecca is a wonderful space holder. I'd chosen to come here. But still, a part of me felt like she'd been dragged here against her will and she was deeply resentful.

The truth is I'd felt this many times before. The idea of gathering with other women – at networking events, spiritual workshops, training programs – was attractive. I signed up enthusiastically. And then wanted to run the moment I arrived.

This time I was giving myself permission to run.

I didn't need to come back for the afternoon session. I'd head to Waterloo and get the train back to Southampton early. I could meet up with Mr H and enjoy some festive celebrations with him.

Safety called.

And then...as I walked through Covent Garden on the way to Waterloo, a busker caught my attention. I stopped. He was about to play his last song and as soon as the first notes sounded out, I knew I had to stay:

"Blackbird singing in the dead of night
Take these broken wings and learn to fly".

I don't tend to have favourites when it comes to music. I mean, who can choose? But 'Blackbird' by The Beatles holds a very special place in my heart.

And hearing it now.
In this moment when I was choosing to separate myself.
Felt like an invitation to reconnect.

I took a deep breath.
I turned around.
And I went back through that door.

I'd love to say that the afternoon session was the most magical experience. The truth is that I still felt uncomfortable. But allowing myself to return and sit with the discomfort, to trust that this was where I was meant to be, activated something in me.

So, why am I telling you this?

Yes, it relates to the fears we can have when it comes to gathering with other women. You'll hear many of the writers in these pages share their own – the sister wound runs deep.

But this event was also important because it's the first

time I met Sarah Lloyd, the sprite-like being who, years later, would invite me to join the Glastonbury retreat that inspired this book.

I sat next to Sarah in the morning session of 'Rise Sister Rise'. We hadn't met before, so when we were asked to do an exercise with the person in the next seat, we smiled nervously at each other; those "do you want to play with me?" vibes bubbling up, wondering if the other person would say "sorry, I've already partnered with her" and being left out.

Fortunately, we did get to play together. As I remember it, the exercise involved exploring the questions:
What am I carrying that isn't mine? (That brought up all the feels for me.)

And,

What would I do if I wasn't scared?

I'd released my first book, *Heal Your Inner Good Girl*, earlier that year and wasn't quite sure what was next for me.

Sarah was still working in corporate PR but wanting to start her own business, so that came up during our exploration.

It was a beautiful few minutes of connection. And then it was over.

I had my "I've got to get out of here" breakdown/ breakthrough.

And I didn't see Sarah again until two years later when we were both at the Mind Body Spirit Festival. I was just about to publish my second book, *UNBOUND*, and was there with my publisher, Sean Patrick of That Guy's House. Sarah was there as the PR for Katie Brockhurst, a fellow TGH author (and contributor to this book!).

I couldn't place Sarah at first. I knew we'd met before, but where?

After a few moments of us trying to figure it out, Sarah realised. "It was the Rebecca Campbell event!"

Talk about magical connections and serendipitous meetings.

From that point on, Sarah and I stayed in touch. She supported me with PR and became one of our first authors at The Unbound Press.

She's a soul sister. And I'm beyond grateful I stayed in the room long enough to meet her.

Over the years I've learned that even when I feel uncomfortable in the company of other women (perhaps especially when I feel uncomfortable), the opportunities for connection and magical unfolding are rich.

Whether the gatherings are HUGE...(being in a New York theatre with 600 other women at Mama Gena's School of the Womanly Arts Mastery Program was intense!)...

...or small, like the Glastonbury retreat, the feelings can run as deep and the experience can be just as transformational.

If we can allow ourselves to trust. And be present.

I still often feel like running whenever I'm gathering with other women. (I pulled over to send a text on the way to meet Sarah and the other retreaters on the way to Glastonbury and a part of me wanted to turn around and go home).

The thought of being with people known and unknown, to let myself be seen and heard, even after years of being on this path, can feel terrifying.

One of the reasons I'm so passionate about creating community and sisterhood is that if I'm holding the space, I have to show up. Running away isn't really an option when you're the one who's invited people to gather.

And it's one of the reasons I've come to love collaborative books. Women coming together not just on the page, but in the process. Navigating our way, each contributing a piece, allowing ourselves to be seen and heard, together and individually.

Different voices.

Different energies.

Different perspectives.

Alchemy.
As we begin this journey together now, unbound one, if you resonate with those feelings of trepidation, discomfort and downright fear when it comes to gathering with other women, please know you are not alone. I'm sure you'll see yourself from different angles, familiar and unfamiliar, in these pages.

In the first collaborative book we published at The Unbound Press, *#2020VISION*, I invited the reader to imagine being in circle with the contributors. Shakti Farts feels different.

As you read on now, I invite you to imagine you're at an event or retreat with each of the writers. Perhaps you end up sitting next to Em and she tells you her story? You meet Sarah in the queue for the loo, sharing your mutual frustration that there are NEVER enough toilets in the Ladies (but at least it gives you plenty of time to chat). Pausing to make a cup of tea, you find yourself in the kitchen with Kathy. Throughout the day you make connections with each of the women who've contributed to this book. And as night falls, you gather around the fire with all of them, drinking red wine (or astral tea), belly laughing and Shakti farting together. Soul sisters.

You are welcome here, magical one.

Always, unbinding.

Nicola Humber

Founder of The Unbound Press
www.theunboundpress.com

Contents

A Vision of Raw Human Connection

by Sarah Lloyd

We were in the kitchen tent feeding our faces on houmous, crisps and dips; splashing red wine into huge wine glasses on the gigantic oak table that stood in the middle of our kitchen.

Yolandi was counting the number of carrots in the veg basket: "OK, who has eaten my fucking carrot?" she teased. (*Yolandi is a blue-haired, kaftan wearing South African who likes to play and say "fuck" a lot! She is also deeply connected to the Star beings and is our guide on such matters.*)

"I haven't!" shouted Kathy, who was reclining on the cosy pink sofa at the far end of the kitchen tent, wearing huge black glasses in an effort to keep the hayfever at bay. (*Kathy is an angelic blonde beauty, a breathwork teacher and has been journeying with me for 4 years now. She is from 'Oop Norf' and says it how it is – which I love her for.*)

Cue raucous, guttural laughing from the four women stood around me. It was what I would call a 'mum joke'.

Earlier that day, we had followed our intuition and instead of shopping before we arrived at our base camp in Glastonbury, we decided to check out the facilities and shop based on what storage/cooking space was available to us.

I am glad we did, because I had visions of buying pizzas and chucking them in the oven for ease...Huge assumption to be made because we were staying on a beautiful campsite that was conscious of its footprint on Mother Earth. Iceboxes and pan-based cooking, and so it is.

Three of us had landed early: me, Katherine (*graceful, tall, dark-haired beauty – an ex-film producer who offers embodiment coaching*) and Nicola (*rebel leader of The Unbound Press and space holder extraordinaire*), so we popped down to the local supermarket and wandered round the fruit and veg aisles, trying to remember the orders, likes and preferences of those joining us for the week.

Knowing energy work and essentially BEing is hungry stuff, we decided to stock up on veg and carbs, with a healing dose of red wine (as my guides suggested and due to the fact it's full of antioxidants).

In full mum mode, I asked Katherine and Nicola how many carrots we thought we'd need: "Do you think six...that's one each?"

Nicola responded, totally deadpan: "That should cover it, as long as no one eats my carrot!"

The delivery of this line is what did for us – both Katherine and I locked eyes and burst out in a loud, hooty, witchy cackle...the magic had begun!

The dreaming of this magical collaboration of souls began back in November 2020, whilst we were in the depths of pandemic nonsense. I had a nudge from the universe to organise a gathering in Glastonbury. It stemmed primarily from wanting to meet the community of amazing souls that I worked with, either clients or those in my Connecting the Dots Membership.

My soul was literally shouting that this needed to happen.

At points it didn't seem like we would be able to pull it off, what with all the patriarchal government restrictions. But I released complete attachment and knew in my heart that it would materialise. That this work was sacred and needed to happen.

This vision felt like it was very different to other retreats I had organised and attended.

This gathering had the vibration of a festival.

A gathering of souls in a field. I kept getting shown a vision of that scene in the film 'Gladiator' where he is in his dream sequence walking through the long grass. That music track made it on to our retreat playlist too.

Simple. A space for BEing over DOing.

So, I set the intention that we would gather in June 2021 – which, as we know, intention is the force behind any magic.

I knew once I had the venue booked, I could allow everything else to fall into place. I knew it couldn't be a building or retreat centre in the town, that insight was very clear – in my body I knew we needed to be outside for some reason. So, I was guided to look at campsites around the area and stumbled upon Banbury Meadow quite by accident. It was when I spoke to Lou, the owner, who told me that the Meadow was an important part of the Glastonbury Zodiac and had connections to Egypt, that I knew the land was calling to us.

Days after sharing that the gathering was coming together, like magic, six sisters shared that they would love to join.

Just to be clear, I didn't see this as 'my' retreat; it was always referred to as a collaboration from the get-go.

This was the guidance: there were to be no 'leaders' or 'pedestals', no hierarchy in any way.

We talked into exchanging offerings, wisdom shares, places we could visit. We were very careful to not organise or set specific agendas outside the dates we had booked our space.

At times, I felt a sense that I needed to be doing more, marketing it more, shouting about it more, caught up in the old ways of doing things. I recognise now it was because I was trying to make it bigger – to capture the festival vibe I had felt – to chase the old habits of what success looks like (money, people, more, more). And of course, there is plenty of time for that in the future...I realise now we have, after all, got to start somewhere.

In fact, I had started trying to turn it into a proper retreat with catering and more tents and more people. It was only when Lou said that due to restrictions, she couldn't go full on retreat mode, I realised I had been holding my breath.

It was the break I was looking for.

I realised I didn't want to organise more than I had to.

That we are all responsible for our own journey, and here again I was being human and trying to control things.

And it wasn't just me. Once I knew we only had space for essentially six bodies, eight at a push if we were to share, it made things so much easier. I was able to say to those wanting to join us maybe for a day, but still on the fence about coming (because leaving family and homes after a pandemic lockdown was a real thing, they really did a number on us) that we could have people join us, but not sleep on site. It took the control away and allowed more people to commit to one day or two days.

This, I realise, was a big lesson for me – in surrendering, and in taking small steps.

So, back to the retreat and the comfort of our sofa in the kitchen tent – women draped over each other, oracle decks scattered, my 'smelly box' of incense and smoking paraphernalia – because who doesn't enjoy an astral tea spliff?

What I see now is there was a framework of sorts that allowed us to flow within. Our deep conditioning has us creating boxes for us to sit in, to make us feel safe. Our conditioning also wants us to fill those boxes to ensure we are being as efficient as possible. One thing I am realising is we can have both. We can have that container to keep us safe – in this case, our physical space – in the hiring of the yurts and the field for a period of time.
AND we can create within that space our freedom.

Part of this work as we unravel the conditioning of our past is confronting those things that kept us small. The shadow work has you slinging mud at the patriarchy because they did this to us. But what I am seeing more and more as I dive into myself is there are some very good aspects of the 'masculine energy' of DOing.

The feminine energy of BEing has been non-existent for many of us. The idea of stopping to look out the window to watch the rain is classed as daydreaming and not constructive. The idea of doing nothing is something many of us struggle to do, because really, when are you ever doing nothing...or perhaps that's just the Virgo in me? I digress. The realisation that this is the time when the best ideas come to us cannot often be quantified.

The beauty of becoming conscious of the two sides to us is, I believe, about loving both aspects and embracing the goodness in both – finding the balance, the space between, the bridge.

We as a group spent a lot of time unravelling some of the 'shoulds' and 'need tos'. We were the anti-agenda retreat – the 'do fuck all' retreat. We joked about it. And whilst we didn't sit around with our PowerPoint presentations, we did talk into our businesses, our fears, our wounds, our ideas.

On our first evening we sat round the campfire getting stoned, drinking red wine, watching the sunset, talking about our stories. Stories of how we met our partners, what our experiences in life before our awakening was like. How we had interacted with other women – we got vulnerable.

At one point in that first evening, my little girl-self decided to show up.

The one who used to give her sweets away or buy others drinks at the bar so she could win friends. She decided to voice her fears. And she asked if she had "done enough" and "if there was more she could be doing?" – a veiled "do you like it, is it OK?...Please be OK".
This part of me used to get shut down with a "*Don't be silly – what are you on about?!*" type response – basically, "*shut the fuck up and get a drink down you*".

My friend Kathy heard and felt that vulnerability and looked deep into my eyes and said, "The little girl in me sees the little girl in you". It was a deeply profound moment of acceptance.

I felt my entire nervous system relax; my little girl slipped off sated and happy.

There were lots of these moments throughout our gathering together, moments of clarity and healing. Belly laugher, tears, snuggles and the fiercest of hugs...and a whole lot of energy or 'Shakti' shifting through us (or 'Shakti farts', as we laughingly coined them).

It was a unique experience for me, being completely in a bubble of love like that. Even when other sisters joined us on the third day, it just felt like the most natural and loving of spaces. The new energy brought new perspectives and insights, and just widened our circle in the most gentle of ways.

No judgement, no sniping, no competing for the limelight – just a sense of feeling held by the group.

I say this, as in the past I could always feel an undercurrent in certain situations – the feeling that someone was sizing up your efforts and thinking they could do better, the conversations behind cupped hands.

I also acknowledge in the past I had worn both of those hats, but it seemed that aspect of myself was either completely blissed out or perhaps at long last she had gone. I could put it down to Kathy's response to me on the first night, or the magical breathwork session that we held on the second day, or just the acceptance that aspect of myself was welcome and so no longer dominated the limelight.

Every other sister who attended the retreat (and those who couldn't be there in person but were celebrated in spirit) we realised, whilst giggling in our bliss bubble, we had met through the power of social media. Some of us had journeyed together for a few years on the same path, rocking and rolling through similar challenges - and some of us had connected during our time in our homes, the sonars reaching out to connect our soul fam who were scattered all over the country.

All I know is that this week for me was one of the most transformational weeks I have experienced in a while.

It showed me what is possible. How powerful the Circle is. How powerful the Mother energy is.

That we can exist in sisterhood, with no agenda, in pure love...as long as each of you have your own carrot.

About Sarah Lloyd

In the media and PR business for 23 years, Sarah Lloyd quit her global corporate role in 2017 in a bid to be a master of her own and to bring a better balance to her life, leading her to create a more magical approach to publicity. An intuitive, angel communicator and Reiki Energy Master herself, she specialises in working in 'flow' so has thrown the PR rule book out the window.

Her mission is to teach and guide others to share their stories, without fear, on their terms.

Specialising in her own brand of magic-based, conscious PR and communications, her Alchemy strategy sessions help to ignite the fire within, acknowledge blocks and help to transmute all that has held clients back from stepping up and sharing their mission and purpose.

She classes Merlin and Mary Magdalene as her spiritual counsel, and in March 2020 her book *Connecting the Dots – A Guide to making Magic with the Media* was published via The Unbound Press. In 2020 she became a judge in the annual Soul & Spirit Awards. You can find more about Sarah's offerings here:
www.indigosoulpr.com

The Circle Wounds

by Yolandi Boshoff

That moment when you walk into a room full of beautiful souls and you know you know them. You know you have journeyed with them many times before and you get to meet again.

Your heart swells with love and remembering at that moment; you feel a deep camaraderie and connection that you can't explain to anyone else.

You know that energetically there are threads running between each and every one of you. Some of you made contracts to meet again, some of you have debts to settle or old wounds to sort out. But all of you have come together for a reason.

And very often we get swept up in the love and light of retreats, we have those moments where we all want to work together towards the mission that we all feel so deeply in our bones. But deep inside there are things that we must understand so that we don't sabotage the mission.

Yes, I know this sounds horrible and I know that all of us have that deep remembering of being together, but we must also look at what happened in those moments when things fell apart and our idyllic view of Circle was shattered – because this was a deep reality that we all want to gloss over and forget.

When we meet people, our energies meet – like when you walk into a room and you feel comfortable with some people and uncomfortable with others – that is your energies coming together and they either embrace or there is friction.

So, in the case of the embrace, that is an easy one to navigate: we walk towards them, see ourselves in their eyes and we know that this is a connection that we can relish and delve deeper into. We remember working together, holding space for each other and cheering each other on in those lives gone past.

But that moment of friction, of the uncomfortable, that moment of distrust when you meet someone – how do you deal with that? When deep inside of you something is telling you that you can't fully connect with this human, you don't hug quite as hard or look into their eyes properly. You know something is amiss.

Well, that, dear one, is where the unravelling of the Circle Wound needs to start. Because, you know what – energy does not lie. Your body and how you feel when you meet someone does not lie.

So, let's look at what happened to us in ancient times.

When we as women were all running around in the good old cave man days, we used to have to fight for a man. We needed to survive, so we wanted one that was a good hunter so he could provide for us and our children that we would bring into this world. But there weren't that many of them, right – Jo the muscle man was there, Ed the fairly competent hunter with a strike rate of about 70% was there and then there was Tom, the nerdy one who was really clever at designing structures, but he could not hunt for shit. And then there was Anne, Mary and me. We would all be there knowing exactly what we needed to survive. Even though the three of us would be in the fields picking berries together or doing the washing by the river, the deepest of love running through our veins for each other, there was something that would override all of that - our desire to survive. Our instinctual nature to want to procreate and make sure the children born would be able to survive in this harsh world.

So, what happens - we move swiftly towards that space of survival of the fittest or in this case, survival of the slyest. We would do anything in our power to get the strongest man. We would lie, cheat and hurt each other. Why? Because we don't want to starve to death...

This is where it all started. And yes, of course there was community, but when we got into the depths of winter and everyone had run out of berries and dried meat, who would go on to make it to the next spring equinox? The one with the strongest man who would be tenacious enough to go out in the storm and look for food.

Being human has always been a race against survival. Being on this Earth plane and working with the idea of Maslow's Hierarchy of Needs, for instance - the bottom two tiers, our physical needs and our safety, always overrides anything else. And once those are established and working well for you, you can start delving into love, belonging, your self-esteem and finally, into self-actualisation.

But so much of our lives are intwined with the concept of survival and fear runs deep through the middle of this. So, when we start living from that place of fear, we disconnect from the essence of humanity and love. Fear makes you focus on staying alive. The age-old fight or flight tendencies kick in and it is each man for himself. We lose our ability to show empathy or to care because all we are doing is trying again not to die! We move out of our heart space and back into instinct.

So fast forward a few thousand years to the witch hunts.

We love to be in circle; again, this is an instinctual need of most humans. We want to belong and fit in, and it all makes us feel safe. But in the times of the witch hunts you chose a circle of women that might have been a bit weird, a bit different, holding ideals and beliefs that did not conform to the norm of society. You didn't really fit into anything that the church and the fearful inhabitants of the village felt was the right mould.

And so, when the decrees came that were designed to weed out the weird ones, the ones who did not fit in or try to fit in, that was when the sisterhood wound really started to show itself to us in all its glory.

Imagine you had to make a choice between your best friend or your child – who would you choose? Imagine if you were presented with an opportunity to survive if you turned on one of your circle sisters? What would you honestly do?

So, think about this: society has been designed to make those who fit in feel safe. I always see it as a bull pen, and you get to walk in there and hang out with everyone else in there. Once you are in, you all get to wear the beige clothes, have the same hairstyles, read the same books and learn the same rules. But inside this space there is no room for people with brightly-coloured clothes or hair. There is no room for people who go against the rules or want to think outside the box. This little cage is created so that the whole world stays in line, and no-one goes a bit mental and creates things that might set their minds and spirits free. And if you are in that bull pen you are also warned against the colourful mad ones; you are so indoctrinated by the powers that be, through your schooling and churching and non-living that you believe every single word of what you are told.

But then one day as you are staring out of the cage, you see her running, you see her laughing in the big meadow of flowers, with her colourful clothes and her free spirit and bare feet. You see her there without any attachment to what is right or wrong as deemed by the powers that be. She is just like a butterfly, and you start wondering what that would be like: "*how would it feel to allow myself to be not here?*" But deep inside you have that voice, the one that tells you she is not good, she does not fit in, she might hurt and upset the perfectly curated structure that is in place and when it all falls apart you won't be safe. You might die...

But what if that little voice inside just won't stop, what if the curious side of you just won't be quiet and let it go? Would you be willing to give up feeling safe? Would you be willing to start exploring you – what you might like, what you feel like and how you want to live?

So, let's step back into that room again, the one you walked into right at the beginning, the one where you saw all those amazing souls. And let's go to that moment where you need to hug one person who makes you feel uncomfortable, when you get that feeling of not connecting, that feeling that something is not right.
Imagine that person now in front of you. Step back and look at them, really look at them. Who is she? Think about all those things popping into your head right now: you might feel like she is slightly insecure, and that she overcompensates in some way to get people to like her. Or maybe you think she is way too loud and obnoxious. Maybe you think she is bossy or aloof.

Whatever you are thinking about her right now, I want you to stop. I want you to imagine why she might be acting like this.

The insecure one standing in front of you, maybe she has suffered years of emotional abuse from a mother who never held her and made her feel safe. The loud one was never heard or acknowledged as a little girl and she needed to always shout to be heard, she just craved a little bit of attention and acknowledgement for the awesome human that she is. The bossy one had no sense of security growing up, she needed to look after an entire household because her mother could not hold it all together and so her control freak tendencies are the only way she holds it all together herself without falling apart.

Now I want you to stop again and step back a little further. Look at yourself. This person triggering that feeling of uncomfortableness deep within you – what is actually going on within you? Deep inside you, are you dealing with insecurities, you also need attention and acknowledgment, or you just want to let go but you can't? Is she showing you parts of yourself that you try to hide or run away from?

That moment that you realise that it's not her, but it is just you. It's always you...She is presenting you with an opportunity to meet yourself there. You can lean into that uncomfortableness and allow yourself to connect with this person. You two might have a shared medicine that will bring itself to light as you spend time talking and connecting.

But our fears of stripping ourselves bare and really looking so often prevent us from connecting deeply. And by realising we all go through this; every single person in the world meets other people who make them feel uncomfortable on some level. This is totally normal.

So, if you go back to that part of us that is still healing from a time where we needed to turn our backs on each other to survive and stay alive, you start to understand why we are all scared to deeply connect with others around us. Why we are scared to step into circles or why we feel we need to protect our circles. Those wounds run so deep.

And this was a way of the patriarchy to force us to turn on each other; it was a way to force us to break the deep bonds that we as humans in circle hold between us. When we step into those circles and allow ourselves to connect on a deep and vulnerable level, we open up brand new fields of energy, power and consciousness and that scares the shit out of them.

As we evolved and realised the power in community and standing together, we tapped into that collective power that we are deeply connected to. When the priestesses started to gather and connect to the Great Mother, that was when magic started happening. Circles of humans supported, loved and held each other.

But what circles also offer us is an opportunity to find our true authentic selves again. By connecting with those around you on a deeper level, you get to see parts of you that you did not even know and parts of you that you never imagined was possible. Our energies meeting in circle forms a melting pot of magic. By allowing ourselves to be in circle, with an open heart, supported and loved, we tap into some beautifully unseen parts. Those gorgeous Souls sitting around you can inspire you; open your eyes to you again.

So now as we have entered this new era, as we are slowly stepping over the threshold into this new Golden Age of Aquarius, what would happen if we found strength, unity and self again in circle?

What would happen if you realised that by healing your inner wounds, your connection with others in circle can be much deeper? The more we heal ourselves, the more we will realise that we can stand together. There will no longer be a need to backstab or wound or harm others with our words and our actions. We will realise that open hearts lead to honest communication and sharing of our fears and our vulnerability. We will realise that this is where our power lies again.

The biggest power lies within you. Creating a consciousness of unity within yourself is where it all starts. The unity that you create within will ripple out. The unity that you feel within yourself creates a space of peace and acceptance. And when you are floating around the world surrounded by that energy, you invite beautiful humans into your space to connect. You give yourself and those that you meet an opportunity to be shown the deep shadow parts that need healing and love.

This amazing retreat and time spent with these gorgeous humans made me realise how many little insecurities I still carried within me. It made me realise that the next time I am presented with an opportunity to connect deeply with other people in a sacred space, that I will endeavour to open my heart and be as vulnerable as I can possibly be at that moment.

Looking back over my life, I realise that the humans that triggered me most on my journey also helped me heal huge issues in my life and often they ended up being my Soul Family.

So, if you are still walking around trying to make sense of the people in your life who wounded you and made you close your heart, take a moment. See them for who they are, see them for the gorgeous souls that they are. See yourself as a gorgeous soul. All we are trying to do here on this planet is to get back to real human connection, so don't let your wounds and their wounds stop you. Never let it stop you. Life is too short to miss out on potentially epic new pathways that can take you deeper into who you are and deeper into love.

All you ever have is one moment. Make it count, make your connections count. Step back into Circle and heal your wounds...

About Yolandi Boshoff

Yolandi is a Lightworker, Starseed, Spiritual Coach, Author and Healer, with a passion for travel, sacred sites and spiritual adventure.

She teaches clients from more than 35 countries across the world how to listen to their inner guidance and return to the essence of their Divine Souls. She does this through DNA Activations, Light Language Healings, Akashic Record Readings, Soul Channelling and Coaching.

She is passionate about working with Mother Gaia in her role as a Dragon Priestess and Grid Keeper and promotes this work through 'Project Earthwork', a collaboration of Souls doing sacred work supporting and loving the Great Mother.

She also shares her teachings through her book (The Starseed Sacred Circle), radio show (The Soul-Led Revolution), podcast (The A to Z of Spirituality), YouTube channel, group meditations, workshops and retreats.

You can find more information about working directly with Yolandi on **www.divinesoul.me**

Sacred Sisterhood, Shakti Farts & Safety To Be Seen

by Em Mulholland

"Hell, yes! Definitely count me in!"

I believe that those were the words (or similar) I uttered to Sarah Lloyd back in 2020 when she first shared her thoughts about organising a retreat in Glastonbury for the following June. I'm pretty sure that the rollercoaster of life amidst a pandemic then got even crazier for most folk, before all of a sudden it got to a couple of months beforehand and reached the point where Sarah mentioned the retreat again.

Having been completely caught up in my own little bubble within my home's four walls, I could feel the 'Glastonbury niggle' in my belly starting to writhe as the lyrics to Queen's inimitable 'I Want to Break Free' burst forth in my brain every time I thought about it – but by the same token, the reality of actually being away from home for a few days after well over a year of movement being restricted was just a tad daunting. I realised that the underlying reticence clashing with the eager clamour to roam freely had its roots in two firm plots of trepidation: the first being the obvious unsettled feeling about being away from Rich and Thomas (my husband and son) after we'd embodied a tightly-knit unit of three throughout the multiple lockdowns – even though the part of my personality that thirsts for independence had been strangled by the restrictions and had in turn left me feeling like an Em-shaped hole through the living room window was on the verge of happening on multiple occasions.

The second twisty unease at that point was the absolute knowing that after the three-night retreat, I would return home and something massive was going to shift or unfold. I groaned inwardly at the mere thought as I reflected upon my previous trips to Glastonbury (aside from to the festival!) and to put it bluntly, there was ALWAYS a shitstorm that happened afterwards. Every. Single. Damn. Time. I don't know what it is about going there, but I'm talking about big life events such as miscarriage, a house move to a different place than intended, leaving behind the only career path I'd known since rolling up at Nottingham Trent University as a fresher with blonde and pink hair and enormous jeans with a chain attached to the pocket (don't ask) twenty years beforehand...yep, we aren't talking small fry life changes here. I wondered what on Earth could possibly happen this time and threw my hands up in surrender as I confirmed to Sarah that I was still definitely a *"hell, yes!"*, for better or worse.

And so fast forward to mid-June and there I was, dashing around the local Matalan after the news that a heatwave was upon the country led me to audit my lockdown lounge attire (translate that as shamefully ancient maternity t-shirts and holey leggings) in the knowledge that it would simply not cut the mustard for the momentous occasion that was socialising with my fellow human beings once more. I think it was around then that "it" hit me: "it" being the little girl inside me piping up in a small yet insistent voice with the *"what if not everyone likes you?"* concerns. Ah. That old chestnut. The inner child work that is seemingly never freaking done, coming to the fore with her inherent shyness and fear of rejection once more. I reminded her that I had spent time with some of the others on retreat in Glastonbury before;

having met Sarah and Kathy Bell in person for the first time on a previous one back in 2019 and having felt at home with them as soon as we had connected online a long time before then – but still. A lot had changed in the world since that retreat, and a lot had changed inside of *me* since then which in turn meant that, in all honesty, I was a little nervous (to say the least).

Rocking up at Sheffield Railway Station where my lift down to Glastonbury with Kathy awaited, I was instantly transported back to the previous retreat where she drove us to Somerset then too. Again, the journey flew by in a flurry of non-stop life chat and laughter, interspersed with the odd service station stop off for highly important snack replenishments and wee purposes. After a slight reroute by a Mother Mary statue on a somewhat barren country road that the sat nav system insisted was our destination, we finally arrived at Banbury Meadow, met with the others and bam, that was it. A few hugs with Sarah, Nicola, Yolandi and Katherine, beds in yurts claimed, confirmation that yes, each one of us had our very own carrot allocated in the veggie stash and several decks of oracle cards/general spiritual paraphernalia splayed across the coffee table later it was safe to say that we were all very much at home.

My inner child felt safe and began to feel even safer as the day wore on into the evening, where we clustered around a fire against the backdrop of the inky pink sunset and consumed our body weights in crisps, cackling uproariously as each sister present laid down the metaphorical burdens she had been carrying either consciously or subconsciously. As the first night together drew to a close, Yolandi placed a singing bowl over my heart and began to bring forth a high, clear, resonant sound. "*It doesn't want to stop*" she whispered to me, our eyes connecting in a gaze of such deep familiarity that it stirred the tendrils of my soul. Both of us had known ever since we first connected on social media that there was something deeper to our paths crossing again in this lifetime, and work that I did with her in the months after our retreat revealed such a richness and depth filled with dragons and past life Earth work together that I couldn't even begin to comprehend it all in that moment, sat by the fireside as the embers began to gently fade away.

That night, I curled up in my nest in the yurt and found my head filled with the usual anxieties about getting a restful sleep – something which had eluded me over the last year or so. I dropped into my body instead, concentrating on the wellspring of love that was reverberating and overflowing in my heart after a day spent in sacred sisterhood and after the singing bowl had done her work there. I became aware of a sense of being suspended in a cosmic womb as I rested my vessel with only the yurt's canopy in between the stars and I, soaking up the potency of the hallowed land that is Banbury Meadow. Drifting into a state of near slumber, Mother Gaia had other ideas as the words "EARTH ACTIVATION" dropped into my head, as loud and clear as the singing bowl had been a couple of hours before. The words repeated over and over until I was finally able to stealth into sleep; a silent promise made that I would not forget them and acknowledging that they were somehow connected to our presence here in Glastonbury at this point in time. All was as it should be.

The following day saw the bonds between the five of us grow deeper after a mind-blowing breathwork session held by Kathy – I still get shivers even when I think about it now. Energy rippled around our circle like quicksilver as each of us released and healed what we needed to and afterwards, slightly giddy, we made our way down to the Abbey to meet the incredible Kdot (Katie Brockhurst) for some lunch and ley line love. The Abbey is one of my all-time favourite places and I don't mind admitting that the energy there sends me a bit funny, in a good way! I caused much mirth as I kept marvelling about how the time was going so fast, high as a kite on the company and Starchild's Astral Tea, and was captured by Sarah on camera as I splayed my arms out wide, face upturned and my inner child shining through for all to witness. She was still feeling safe, loved and seen – it was all good.

I think that night was possibly my favourite one of the trip because by this stage, everyone was visibly ultra-relaxed and I honestly don't think I had laughed that long and hard in a very long time: the phrase *"this is the 'Fuck All' Retreat... because we're doing fuck all!"* was coined, along with the now infamous 'Shakti Fart' (definition: a fart brought on by deep healing, relaxation, laughter, connection and the never-ending supply of crisps) and the idea for this very book that you're holding in your hands right now was joyfully born.

The day after – the Wednesday and the final full day of our retreat – saw the arrival of several new people joining us in hanging out at the meadow. My inner child started to feel a familiar gripping sensation in her belly as a sense of social anxiety began to unfurl and I realised that I couldn't remember the last time I'd physically been in such a big group, in light of the lockdowns that had largely peppered the pandemic. When I scratched beneath the surface, I realised that it wasn't for health reasons that I felt concerned about being in a large group...it was that whole sensation of worrying about not being liked, being judged as lacking and my old tormentor: inadequacy. I watched as these vibrant, beautiful souls spilled into the kitchen/lounge area of the communal tent, their effervescence and their smiles lighting up the space, and I instinctively shrank in on myself. Now, if this had been a night out or a festival, I would have poured myself a large glass of wine and started drinking steadily until I felt a false self-confidence begin to bloom – but it was neither of those types of environment. Every part of me clamoured to be back in Yorkshire with my boys and so I took myself off and FaceTimed them; my husband instantly picking up on my voice and my expression as awkwardness came off me in waves. I wanted to cry as I looked at my son, the longing to hold him in my arms like a visceral force that engulfed me in its vice like grip. Why was I feeling like this? Had anyone given me any reason to by means of their behaviour? No. It was all me, all my lifelong self-esteem shit surging and churning like an angrily erupting volcano or a rampaging bull. Worse still, I was in a group of incredibly intuitive people who would spot this a mile off and quite frankly, that thought made me feel even worse.

Taking deep breaths and stealing off for a few minutes here and there when I needed to, I enmeshed myself in the conviviality that the fresh energy of new additions to a group brings and I found myself curious about these new people I'd only previously connected with via the retreat's WhatsApp group. I was immediately drawn at first to curl up with Zoë: her soul appearing to me like a wise, creative ocean of vivid colours and textures as I admired her breathtaking art prints and as we swapped conversation on deep subjects effortlessly and with an instinctive sense of trust emanating from each of us. I also enjoyed a brief conversation with Rachel, whose radiant smile and all-round vivacious gorgeousness as a person oozed from her like a rich and inviting honey; her very presence somehow making me feel more at ease as I found myself feeling glad she was there. I began to allow little glimpses of myself to become visible again as my subconscious finally caught up with the vibrations of safety and ease that was permeating the group, and I knew in my heart that I would miss the presence of each of these women as we returned to our respective homes scattered around the UK.

The final day of our time together dawned grey after the resplendent peacock-blue skies that had been the hallmark of our retreat. With lingering reluctance, we bade our farewells to Banbury Meadow and its custodians, Lou and Tom, who are two of the nicest, wisest and most interesting people I have had the pleasure to meet – such was the impression they made upon me in a very short space of time. We decamped to the Chalice Well, another place that sets my heart and soul alight thanks to its sacred magic and causes me to beam like the Cheshire Cat, and I found myself sat in the place betwixt and between two of the magnificent yew trees there. The trees spoke softly to me; whispering that "*she who speaks the language of the trees speaks the language of the Earth to those who have the ears to listen*". Chin tilted aloft, I absorbed their wisdom with a quiet acceptance before taking my leave from this deeply and exquisitely special place.

And so it was that I returned home to Yorkshire with a head and a heart full of memories; my soul easeful and lighter after the abundance of laughing and Shakti farting and the treasure chest of new connections spilling its bejewelled and inviting contents joyfully about my energy field. The retreat was exactly what I had needed on so many levels and yes, transformation and shifts most certainly did come about in the form of true, seismic Glastonbury after effect-style. I certainly didn't think that as I came to finish this chapter (having abandoned it after the first 600 words a few months ago because the creative tap turned itself off), I would be working with the magical Nicola as The Unbound Press's first employee and having the pleasure of interacting with some of those from the retreat as part of my actual job! My shamanic path has also noticeably notched itself up a gear: Spirit has made it clear to me that there is no hiding from that aspect of my soul's journey in this lifetime and that the "Earth Activation" the land spoke so loudly and insistently to me of at Banbury Meadow is a huge part of the work I came here to do.

I will always be grateful for the time spent farting and feasting with this group of amazing souls in June of 2021 and how it eclipsed the shadowy anguish of the first part of the year for me. My butterfly wings have shyly unfurled as I now allow myself to be seen, and as I now realise that I don't always have to be actively visible and "putting myself out there" in the world because the glorious technicolour of those wings is here to stay.

About Em Mulholland

Em Mulholland is a Shamanic Practitioner and copywriting Word Doula based in West Yorkshire, England. She left behind life as a practising commercial litigation lawyer in early 2020 and embarked upon her passions of working with energy and words in the midst of her shamanic training and a global pandemic; heeding the nudges of Spirit & her soul and casting aside the cloak of "shoulds" and "musts" dictated by society and her professional life up until that point.

One of Em's greatest loves is working with crystals and she regularly incorporates their messages and medicine into her shamanic sessions, her role as a Celtic Reiki Master and also a Metatronia® Therapist. Additionally, Em discovered her gift of supporting other spiritually-minded folk in sharing their words with the world and so the concept of the Word Doula was born, weaving together the power of energy work and the written word. Em also enjoys writing a quarterly column and supporting Indie Shaman Magazine in her role as columnist and sub-editor.

Em also works as the Operations & Author Relations Assistant for The Unbound Press, a soul-led publishing imprint for magical women, and is a published author in the world of legal academia.

You can find out more about Em's work on Instagram **@one_spiritual_mother**

The Little Girl in Me Sees The Little Girl in You

by Kathy Bell

I am here. I am her. I am she. I am here. I am her. I am she.
I am here. I am her. I am she. I am her. I am here. I am she.
I am here. I am her. I am she. I am here. I am her. I am she.
I am here. I am her. I am she. I am her. I am here. I am she.
I am here. I am her. I am she. I am here. I am her. I am she.
I am here. I am her. I am she. I am her. I am here. I am she.
I am here. I am her. I am she. I am here. I am her. I am she.
I am here. I am her. I am she. I am her. I am here. I am she.

When Sarah first told me about the retreat, my initial reaction was to jump on in say yes straight away – not only because I love Glastonbury, I love Sarah and I love retreats, but because:

I didn't want to be left out.

One of my deepest and most painful childhood memories and my first experience of mistrusting or being hurt by another female was a situation where I was left out and rejected. It has been one of the most impactful events that has defined my decision making when it comes to almost anything throughout my life.

Social events, making friends, behaving in relationships, how I behave in social situations, how I dress, who I am in social settings and even who I present as online: I can safely say this childhood wound shaped me as a child, a teen and a woman.

I didn't know back in January 2021 when Sarah asked me to join her on retreat that I would get to heal this wound, in a field, surrounded by magical women, in the heart chakra of the world. But I did and here is the start of my story.

At the age of 7, I was quite boldly told that I "*didn't belong*" and that I "*needed to go home*."

Yep, it was as blunt as that. I won't dress it up, dramatise it or play it down.

I innocently went with my best friend to another girl's house (who I didn't know) and who lived down the street in order for us to play. We lived on a quaint avenue lined with huge trees. My friend and I had been friends for years as we were born around the same time and had grown up together. There were lots of children (mainly girls) who lived on our avenue, yet we were all syphoned off to different primary schools so didn't all know each other. The avenue was long and the houses seemed to get posher and bigger as you went down it. The girl in question's house was RIGHT at the bottom. Her house was enormous and the garden was beautifully manicured. Part of me already felt out of place. Minutes after arriving, I was outed by the girl whose garden we were in. She point blank told me that she didn't want me in her garden and I needed to leave. Shocked, I had to leave the safety & comfort of my best friend behind and go home, like she told me to.

I wasn't welcome.

I didn't belong.

I needed to leave.

I was ashamed. What would I tell my Mum? Why was I home

so early and why was I crying? Why did my best friend just stand there? Why did this girl not want me in her garden? What was wrong with me?

I felt so incredibly embarrassed, abandoned and hurt. The tears stung my hot, red, embarrassed face and my little legs, filled with adrenaline, carried me quickly home. My mother couldn't understand what was wrong with me or why I was home and I was too embarrassed to tell her. I don't remember the rest of the day or what happened next, but all I know was that at age 7 I got my first hit of the searing pain of jealousy and rejection – and from that moment I hated being left out and it amplified the aloneness I felt as an only (sensitive) child.

I started to feel like I didn't belong in all the social situations I was in and withdrew from my friends; beginning to get jealous of other people who seemed to be naturally accepted in social situations. I was desperately scared of being left out, which only made it more likely. And it became my "thing" – I was so scared of it I was always seeking it out and lo and behold, it always found me. I led a life of "three's a crowd" friendships and was the girl who found out on Monday that everyone went to a sleepover on Saturday.

Other people didn't have a hard time fitting in.

Other people didn't get left out.

It must be me.

I must not belong.

And I carried this around with me for the next 30 years, on high alert in ALL social situations, constantly assessing if I belonged, doing anything, and I mean anything, to fit in and not get left out or thrown out of the party! This looked like agreeing – A LOT. Never arguing or disagreeing or having my own thoughts. Being insanely upbeat and FUN! Going along with the crowd, *no matter what.* It looked like saying yes to every invite even if I didn't want to, excessive people pleasing and sacrificing my values and morals for the acceptance (and safety) of others.

My feminine was wounded and I sacrificed A LOT of myself to be accepted and belong.

And at the time of Sarah organising her retreat, I had been looking into this wound.

Very much aware of my people pleaser tendencies, I had to tune into and use my discernment when saying yes for real to Sarah's retreat.
Did I want to be there because I love Glastonbury and I love Sarah and I love retreats?

Did I want to be there because it was a soul desire, a serendipitous moment in time that I signed up for light years ago?

Or...

Did I want to be there because I couldn't face the pictures on social media and feeling the feeling of not belonging again?

Was I so scared of my wound being triggered that I would say yes to anything?

I wasn't sure based on my track history, so I stewed on it. I asked myself the questions. I questioned my motives. I allowed myself to not know until the last minute.

I eventually said yes – and the reason?

I was starting to feel OK with being left out.

In the space between the invite and me saying yes, my intentions and work around this wound had put in motion a momentum where I was able to root into myself even more than ever before and begin to heal this wound.

I was able to start to reclaim my power and realise my true worth. I was worthy even if my sensitised body detected I was "being left out".

I tended to my wounds and my "high alert" status and connected to the truth:

I was good enough, worthy enough and special enough even if these women gathered and I wasn't there. Even if I felt left out:

I was still loved by God.

I was still part of the sisterhood.

I was going to be OK, there or not there.

So I went – because I love Sarah, I love Glastonbury and I love retreats.

Landing Back Home

I am here. I am her. I am she. I am her. I am her. I am she. I am here. I am her. I am she. I am here. I am her. I am she. And she is me.

Arriving in Glastonbury is always a homecoming for me.

The land feels familiar. The air speaks to my heart. The water soothes my soul. The campfire ignites my spark.

I am born anew each time my feet touch the earth of Avalon. Arriving and meeting Nicola, Yolandi, Katherine for the first time – women who I'd only ever met online – was incredible! Holding them, loving them and laughing with them was magical.

I felt seen and witnessed – it was a familiar feeling that I first experienced on the very first retreat I ever went on with Rebecca Campbell in 2017, and it was a very welcome, familiar feeling. There is something magical about being met by energetically powerful women who you just don't meet in the bread aisle in Tesco, and I think this kind of witnessing only happens on retreats – another reason why they're so special.

Even though we all hadn't met in real life before, we quickly slipped into a relaxed sisterhood vibe brought together by laughter; lots and lots of laughter, mainly brought on by the contents of Sarah's Smelly Box, carrots and red wine – items you don't find on a typical retreat!

As we started to talk openly about our triggers, especially around other women, it was interesting to me to hear and witness these powerful women share similar feelings and experiences to me...and in reflection, this noticing initiated 'The Little Girl in Me Sees the Little Girl in You' poem I'm about to share with you.

On the third day we were to be joined by some other ladies and I was nervous. Online they were confident, exuberant and had their shit together. My little girl was apprehensive: how would their arrival change things? What if the new people joining us changed things up and I got left out?

My fear started to make herself known.

I am here. I am her. I am she. I am here. I am her. I am she. I am her. I am here. I am she. I am here. I am her. I am she. And she is me.

I had these affirmations on repeat in my head.

Then serendipitously, Sarah told me that Rachel (Smithbone, one of the ladies joining us) was deeply nervous about coming and was worried about how she was going to fit in.

I was taken aback. Really? This amazing, exuberant, strong woman was nervous about belonging too?

Hearing that Rachel was nervous made my heart skip a beat. I started to see how it wasn't just me. It wasn't just me that felt insecure in groups.

There had been a shift in me and upon her arrival I met her with my eyes. I met her with my heart. I met her in a totally new way and rather than feel separate from her and making it all about me, I started to see us all as one and made it about US. I went out of my way to make the new arrivals feel welcome: not that I wouldn't have usually, but this was different – I did it from a place of love rather than protecting myself. I felt a shift in my heart space – I was braver. Not chatting to them so they accepted me but I chatted to them so they knew they weren't alone. I saw them through the eyes of my inner child and talked to their inner child...my capacity for compassion had grown.

It wasn't long before I took myself off to find my journal and wrote this poem:

The Little Girl in Me Sees the Little Girl in You

Surprises in Sisterhood

When you can meet another sister with the gentleness and sweetness of your child self, things change

She longer is your enemy
She no longer is your competition

When another woman holds the gaze of your inner child's eyes with her inner child's eyes, there is a grace that flows and a space that is filled

She no longer feels you as a threat
She no longer knows you as a danger

When your child is met and held by another, there is a softness

You melt
You receive
You land
You love

She is you and she always has been
She feels you as you feel yourself
She knows you
She is you

The little girl in me sees the little girl in you

Let's allow them to play, frolic, merge, entwine, support, hold and mother one another

We are wise and elaborate, intricate and complex...

Each one of us carries the magic
We are not alone
We never are
And we never were.

As I read this out loud to the now 10+ group of women, I felt a collective shift.

Thanks to Sarah's relaxed itinerary, smelly box and the 38° heat we had slowed right down, saw one another, heard one another and healed one another's little girls.

Rachel and I sat nose to nose later that day and gazed into each other's eyes. My scared little girl seeing her scared little girl and LOVING each other.

And the magic happened. We healed something that day, whether it was collective or just between our group: we all felt it. Feeling seen, heard and loved on a whole new level. The poem sparked more heartfelt conversations about how we all interrelate as women, how scared and insecure we often feel and how sad it is. Many, many ideas were born that day as our collective hearts softened and welcomed all women into our consciousness of our little girls.

All of you is welcome & "doing" FUCK ALL

As I'm sure you have already read, this particular retreat created by Sarah was different to your normal retreat. There was no planned itinerary, no events, no morning or evening circles, just flow and space and a lot of "fuck all". Sure, there was a loose "plan", but we had copious amount of space where there was nothing planned at all – hence the "Fuck All" label!

And it turned out the "fuck all" was the most magical thing

about the whole week but it was also the hardest part for me!

Naturally a high energy person, I am one for being busy. Couple that with a highly-charged nervous system and the excitement of my maiden out to play in her sacred land, doing "fuck all" was HARD. A lack of a busy structure showed me my edges and made me feel uncomfortable. Every single retreat I had been on up until this point had been jam-packed with events, travel, circles, activities and this one was NOTHING like that. So what would we do? My inquiring mind would ask. It was hard, but I put on my best "I'm OK with that" face and felt my discomfort. My discomfort squirmed and poked me – forward momentum was my thing, yet I was surrounded by women who were OK with stillness.

The first day was OK, maybe even the second day too; by the third day I was itching, but I stayed with it. I stayed with myself – I stayed with the discomfort even though it was awful and at around 3:00pm on the third day I started to feel a shift (it was THAT big I can be THAT specific!). I started to feel OK with being enough just as I was. I started to feel OK with NOT having the forward momentum. I started to feel OK with staying still. I started to feel OK with knowing that I was enough just as I was. I started to feel OK with the stillness. I started to feel OK with ME; with the desire to be busy and the discomfort of not being busy all going on inside of me!

And this is where "all of you is welcome" comes in. This is something I first heard from one of my mentors, Madeline Giles. She said it in a breathwork group and it stuck with me.

In THIS moment (the third day, 3:00pm) when I welcomed all of me, the most magical thing happened: life opened up to me and I was gifted a different level of presence to it. In being given the opportunity to do "fuck all", I had been given the opportunity to welcome all of me – the discomfort and the pain.

And the best part was that I didn't go through this alone. The magical part was that I was able to have this conversation with the other women: Katie, Sarah, Emma, Yolandi, Nicola, Jesse, Zoë, Rosie, Rachel, Katherine, Michelle...they all met my uncomfortable energy with love and kindness and understanding. They MET ME just as I was. They accepted all of me. They saw me and felt my discomfort and held the space for me to work through it.

And this, I think, is one of the most transformational things that can happen on retreat. When we step out of our comfort zone, when we step out of our routine, when we step out of familiarity and everything we are used to – our life of comfort we so desperately create – we are met with an opportunity to feel our discomfort and mostly there is nowhere to go. We don't get a choice, and we face the pain. And in facing the pain and discomfort in a safe space with other women who understand you, life opens. This retreat wasn't just a fun trip away with some friends; it was a life-changing time and space where I got to delve into parts of me that I wouldn't have if I had stayed at home.

I want to deeply thank the women who shared this space with me, who held and loved and accepted ALL OF ME as I stayed with myself so that I could come home to these new parts of me. Thank you. I am here. I am her. I am she and the little girl in me will always see the little girl in you.

I also want to thank Yolandi, Katherine, Nicola, Emma and Sarah for trusting me to hold space for them during my first ever in-person breathwork group session. Thanks to Covid, one of my dreams came true: I trained as a group breathwork facilitator with David Elliot in the early Summer of 2020 – but also thanks to Covid, I never got to share my new training with real life people until the Summer of 2021! So, holed up in a four-bed yurt, the six of us set up space for me to hold a group breathwork session for them and I had never felt energy like it as they started to breathe – it was one of the most moving and special moments of my life and will long stay with me as one of my pivotal moments. I can't thank you all enough for your trust and presence – I love you!

About Kathy Bell

Kathy is an experienced Breathwork Facilitator, Mentor and Author who specialises in holding loving, clear and expansive spaces for you to come home to your truth and integrate your soul's essence into your human reality.

People who work with Kathy are met with love and are given the space, freedom and compassion to be exactly who they are and who they came here to be. Kathy gently empowers her clients to see that being human really is the point, and her practices are woven with the threads of balancing spirituality and humour with grounded, practical wisdom for everyday living.

As a highly sensitive empath on her own journey, Kathy embraces spending time in nature, observing the cycles of Mother Earth and reflecting on the cycles within herself.

Kathy lives with her husband, daughter and two dogs just outside Sheffield in South Yorkshire, England. She has had careers in aviation, high school teaching and trauma-informed resilience building with a specialist not-for-profit organisation before she established her healing practice.

Website: **www.kathybell.uk**

Out Of The Lion's Den And Into The Arms Of Sisterhood

by Katherine Crawley

Being in Glastonbury for me was about being free.

Being free from all daily constraints that so often keep me boxed in, one way or another. Being a mother, being a partner, being a lover, being a space holder, being an entrepreneur.

Whenever I am wearing one hat or the other, there is a tendency to block the flow of the magic that is All of Me.

Being in Glastonbury, on the land, in a group of real, heart-centred women, was a safe space to truly Be All of Katherine; a woman that weaves and dances, laughs and farts, cries and wails, feels and heals; a woman with her feet deeply rooted in the ground, elegantly adorned, heart beating an ancient feminine bloodline of embodied power and wisdom.

So when Sarah first suggested I come to Glastonbury, something deep inside me said YES. You know when you get those deep gut instincts and you have come to a place in your life when you can move beyond the chattering in the mind that wants to hold you back, that wants to keep you in that box, the box that restricts, conditions, squeezes... Yeah, so, when you've found the inner fire to burn down those barriers and follow your gut instincts, which are so divinely guided, you get to jump on a plane from Glasgow to Bristol and go on a wild glamping adventure with a group of extraordinary women.

But of course, there is always a process to get there; the journey is always as important as where you're going, so the saying goes!

Money is not easy for me...Since losing all our financial wealth five years ago in a big fraud scandal, it's been hand to mouth, really. So allowing myself to spend £550 on this trip, something for me, something you could define as indulgent, was a Big One. That yes, even though I had lost all of our money through a misguided investment (trusting my friend of 15 years), I still deserved to spend £550 on me!

But where was I going to find it? It is so hard to write about this, but my soul seems to be guiding me to lay it all bare – because This Is Me. This is the story of me really embodying the boundless love of my soul and not allowing myself to hold back as a result of the constraints of money.

And that moves me to tears, tears of love, of gratitude and of self-compassion.

And, of course, the more I do this, on a day-to-day basis, the more I let go of the guilt and shame and learn to truly own my own abundance and self-worth in this life, the more the money shows up when I need it. And when I embody this vibration, everything feels possible again.

I am deeply blessed with such a beautiful life now, living in a rented cottage on the coast of Scotland, overlooking the sea, the bounty of Mother Earth all around me, two magical boys and a truly beautiful man who holds and embraces all the woman I am.

And looking back now, I know that none of this reality would be mine, had we not lost all our money. Without financial freedom, we had to stick together, we had to learn to truly be with each other, we had to work through it; we couldn't run away because life was asking us to get stuck in and trust in the process and for that I am so deeply grateful.

And this seems to be one of the greatest learnings of all really, that in the depths of the darkness, when life feels like it's falling apart around you, the light shines in in the most unexpected and magical ways.
So the £550 showed up, as I knew it would, because I chose myself, my heart was open and I trusted the universe.

I was going. Now I had to pack!

I was going to a field in Glastonbury and so surely it couldn't be that hard; my husband never understands why it takes me so long to pack. But the truth is there are so many old triggers that come up around clothes, around dressing, around adorning my body with love, creativity and colour. It makes me smile deeply to be able to share through this oh-so-potent lens! Because the world of fashion can be so bloody all-consuming – well, it certainly was for me.

I feel that I was lucky because I always loved dressing. My father had been a really extravagant dresser in his own way, wearing orange blazers, knee-high pink socks with garters, yellow Bermuda shorts and brasses, with outlandish ties and always a Panama hat. He was known for his extravagance and I guess I naturally followed in his footsteps.

But for so many years, I was dressing to fit an image of myself – whether that was a sexy dominatrix luring men by night; a chic, sophisticated businesswoman wining and dining top CEOs and members of government; a trendy Soho-based documentary film producer with a strong message to get out to the world; a yummy mummy or even a radiant yogi – I was always dressing to fit a certain image.

It was exhausting, stressful and deeply judgemental.

And where was I in this whole charade? What about the true expression of Katherine?

In the first instance, I gave up on myself totally. I was so tired of trying, so tired of chiselling myself that I just let everything go. My skin was tired of makeup, my body was tired of clothes. I wanted to disappear into myself so I chose to forget about myself in this way all together.

It was some years later, after a time of deep healing and transformation that took me through the pain and undoing of miscarriage to a place of deep womb awakening, that things began to shift. I was able to forgive myself for the many years of abuse I had put my body through and hence began to know this temple of mine with a whole new depth of tenderness and love.

I discovered the gift of essential oils, feeling and allowing the pleasure of touch as it awakened the felt sense experience of being in this body. I started to wear rich and vibrant colours that enhanced the vibrations of my chakras. In essence, my relationship to dressing shifted away from a necessary piece of image-building to a deeply ceremonial honouring of this feminine body that is mine in this lifetime.

Now, I am more and more drawn to being naked, because my nakedness feels like the freest, most empowered expression of me. And interestingly, there was lots of sisterly calling out to each other in the chat before we went to Glastonbury to get naked and roll around in the mud. So it's obviously not just me! There seems to be a collective calling to strip off all the layers and smear our bodies in the rawness of the Earth, sounding deep, guttural calls of ancient primordial life.

Sadly, we didn't quite get there...next time, though. You coming?

So, embarking on my journey to Glastonbury, I felt deeply embodied and centred. There were no masks to put on; this was about being All of Me. I felt a childlike excitement that made me smile deeply.

And so meeting Sarah for the first time, in the flesh (we had spent many an hour journeying together online, but this was the first real human hug), was like being reunited with one of my beloved childhood friends. It felt so snug and comfortable and so, as we giggled our way from Bristol Airport to the setting of our gathering, my soul smiled. My whole body, at a cellular level, smiled. I was 'at home' with this beautiful woman, totally safe to 'Be Me'.

And as one woman after another landed in the space that day, the smile in my heart just grew and grew.

There were of course little moments of trepidation as each of these amazing women, radiant and powerful in their own light, arrived: moments of "*would they like me?*", "*would we connect?*" and "*would there be old triggers of competitiveness that would arise?*"

But again and again, as I breathed into the heartbeat of my womb and rooted myself into the Earth, supporting myself to show up without fear, expectation or judgement, I was met with the same beautiful open-hearted truth.

I often find being around more than a handful of people stifling, like there is just too much interference in my energy field that I start to feel like the space around me is closing in and I am drowning.

But this was the opposite – it was all about breath and for me that is not only about taking responsibility for the depth of my own breath, but also about cultivating a deep connection with the Earth under my feet and the air that I am breathing.

And Banbury Meadow was so present in this experience for me. I have always had a deep connection to nature, but the depth of my relationship with Mother Earth has recently developed a whole new level of awareness.

It is through knowing myself as a woman, an embodied woman, deeply in love with the gift of life in this body that the voice of the Earth speaks to me and through me more and more potently.

I know that might all sound a bit nuts! But it has been my experience that as we remember who we are as women, we remember that we are one with our Earth. She is us and we are her. I suppose in a way, it's like finding God. And that definitely feels weird to say! But you just don't feel alone anymore, you don't feel separate and you equally don't feel so all-important as you know, deep in your womb, that you are an expression of her.

And that was so alive for me at Banbury Meadow. The magic of how Lou had established these beautiful yurts so in harmony with the nature of the land. There were narrow paths of mown lawn weaving through the long grasses, full of crickets and butterflies; there was a lake humming with dragonflies of indigo and gold and there were the most fabulous compost loos I have ever had the pleasure of sitting on.

The energy of the land was so alive, strong and peaceful, and I could just feel that pulsing up through the soles of my naked feet as I took time for me.

I was in a lot of pain in my hip and lower spine when I arrived. Something which is rare for me, being a yogi, but I had had an intense session with a healer the week before and he had opened my eyes to a new awareness that was really painful to receive. And I knew my body was responding to that; I had gone into total spasm.

But as soon as I sat by the lake, I could feel the land holding me, healing me, whispering "it's safe to let go". And so when we gathered for Kathy's beautiful breathwork session on Day Two, I was ready to let it all flow through me: the tears, the pain, the deep, deep release. Can you imagine lying next to someone you've only just met, grunting, wailing and pummelling?! Our society would have us believe that's all a bit crazy – dangerous, even!!

Well, let me tell you, it's amazing and it works. After an hour of what you might call 'big feels' the pain was gone, just like that – after days of heavy painkillers, it was all gone.

And every woman played a part in that healing process for me, just as I was playing a part in theirs. Beyond the confines of the personality, in that raw flow of energy, heart open, so much can move and transform.

Magical light is the energy field that grew and grew around us, through us, of us. The sunsets around the fire, the stillness, the love, the laughter, ohhh so much laughter.

Rachel didn't arrive until the last day, but I knew the moment I laid eyes on her that I had known her my whole life. We held each other womb to womb with this deep sense of remembering each other and then we smiled.

And this kind of laughter is not as we experience it, day to day, it's not an "oh, that's funny" kind of laughter, it's belly laughter, it's like a deep sense of letting go. When you know you are seen and received and you know it's safe to get naked, then your body relaxes in a way it hasn't in most of your lifetime, and then you laugh, truly laugh – a deep, letting it all go and farting kinda laugh!

And so the experience of meeting new women for the first time was changed for me over the course of those four days – forever. I realised that it was not about a meeting of the minds, but rather a meeting of the souls. And that was not a mental experience, it was a felt-sense one: a deep stirring of the senses, gentle whispers and big full-body smiles.

Meeting Nicola felt like watching a romantic sunset on a tropical island, the last rays of rich warmth bathing my skin and the sweet smell of jasmine wafting on the breeze. She felt opulent, sensual and wild.

Meeting Kathy felt like stealing into a forbidden cake shop, full of the most deliciously tantalising cream cakes, red velvet cupcakes and chocolate éclairs. Kathy felt like lemon sherbet, so full of the tingling aliveness of life, all in and mischievous.

Em felt like magical woodland, ancient trees deeply rooted, the smell of pine strong on the breeze and the touch of soft green moss on my skin. She felt vast and calm.

Meeting Yolandi felt like walking through a Bedouin village: hot, mysterious, exciting, something ancient and wise at every turn. Yolandi felt like a candlelit ceremony of prayer and song honouring the divine gift of life.

Zoë felt like a rainbow, a powerful expression of colour and movement. Michelle like a rambling rose, beautiful, sweet, as well as thorny and fierce and then last, but by no means least, there was Katie.

Being with Katie was like jumping on a wild mustang and riding hard across the vast open plains; so passionate, so intense, so alive. I could have spent a lifetime talking to Katie, especially on the sacred soil that is the site of Glastonbury Abbey.

I could feel the potency of that land channelling through us both, both of us so open to receiving that ancient, timeless, earthly wisdom. We had been there before. The time we spent diving into each other's psyche was beyond space and time and I could almost see the rippling out effects of it; the drumbeat of our souls calling up the embodied power of women to remember and to rise again.

And so there we all were, we had arrived. Now what?

And now I just want to laugh and giggle and fart! Because it was like we had done all the work we had come to do and now we could play.

We had each allowed ourselves the space, negotiated ourselves gracefully and lovingly away from our husbands/partners and kids, showed up in the most authentic way and integrated with each other freely and lovingly.

And I don't know about you, but in my life experience of being a woman, in relationship with other women, mostly in work environments as well as in extended family settings, this is no easy feat. In my experience, there has always been so many layers of false persona that take over, creating tension and judgement; the old stories about who I should and shouldn't be leading the way, making meetings uncomfortable, unsafe and sometimes really upsetting.

It has taken me years to understand what goes on for us when we walk into a room of new people. And going into that would be long indeed, but having spent years unpicking it, I feel like a little nugget of wisdom I can share is this: *Before you embark, pause, take a deep breath, deep down into your belly and change the story.*

Know that you are not walking into a lion's den full of bitches on heat that will eat you alive in order to safeguard their place of power in the pack. Know that your central nervous system does not need to go full throttle into your 'fight or flight' response in order to survive. Know that this is an old story, just a story, and that it no longer serves you.

Take a few more deep breaths and remember your heart, listen to her beating, let her rhythms fill you up and write a new story. A story of love and deep acceptance, a story of safety and light, a story of freedom and joy, a story of sisterhood, a story of Shakti farts and belly laughs.

And as for the Laughter Yoga story, well, I'll let one of my sisters tell that one...!

About Katherine Crawley

Katherine's passion lies in reconnecting All Women to the true essence of Being All Woman.

Guided by her own journey through the abusive distortions of self-harm, drug and sex addiction, the shame and guilt of losing all her financial wealth through fraud and then the deep sorrows and grief of abortion, miscarriage and parental loss, Katherine has been challenged again and again to strip back the layers and go deeper, finally awakening to the true wisdom and power of her feminine soul.

Drawing on her deep knowledge of yoga and Yoga Therapy for women's health, alongside her intimate experience in Awakening Women's Facilitation, Katherine mentors women around the world to step back from the relentless drive and self-doubt of their personas and awaken to the wisdom and power of Being All Woman.

As founder of AllKatherine, Katherine is also a passionate advocate of the WombWisdom movement.

With a background in international advertising sales and feature-length documentary producing, Katherine has travelled the world, interviewed princes and presidents, raised philanthropic investment on supper yachts, premiered at Sundance and lunched with stars.

Co-producer of award-winning documentaries, *KZ* and *Black Gold.* Producer and Co-Director of *Fezeka's Voice*, available on Netflix

Email –krcrawley@hotmail.com
Mob +44 7418 095 622
www.facebook.com/katherine.crawley.9

Return To Embodiment

by Katie Brockhurst

When Sarah told me about her idea to create a kind of retreat-meets-mini-festival for connecting and collaborating with our contemporaries, our clients, co-creators and connections in Glastonbury, it was a full body "YAY!"

Glastonbury has been my home for three years now, a sacred and special place that I am still getting to know and understand more as each day goes by, living here in the midst of it all. The vortex. The zodiac. The heart chakra. The Isle of Avalon, with its fairy portals, access to the astral planes and ancestors. It has mythology and magic weaving many mysteries across town from the Tor to the Abbey. The Michael and Mary lines merging the energies of the divine masculine and divine feminine, alongside the red and white springs, which carry their water and light throughout the town for its residents and visitors. For a small town in the middle of the English countryside in Somerset, there is a lot going on here. It is a multi-dimensional place of pilgrimage and to have the party gather here felt only fitting for this first time with our connected comm~unity.

Community. Ah, now this is a word that gets bandied around a lot in the online business and marketing space. As our group's resident *Social Media Angel* working within the spiritual wellbeing space for over a decade, I am hardwired to recognise when these marketing cliches come along. A word like 'community' has in recent years become harder to trust, as it is spun into sales copy alongside other favourites such as 'authenticity' and 'vulnerability'. I hold my hands up as someone that has used them. But these words, these concepts, become so overused to the point where they lose their meaning. Yet these concepts are so incredibly powerful when being used in and for their true essence.

The qualities of Community ~ Authenticity ~ Vulnerability were all very present during this retreat, indeed by the bucketload – which I am sure you are picking up on in the other chapters. I was only with the ladies during the day, because of living so close to the meadow where the group were all staying. Yet despite popping in and out, I saw all three qualities in play in the most natural, beautiful and organic of ways. I think this was one of the most defining things about this gathering for me. We were not trying to be authentic or vulnerable with one another, nor even trying to create community. It was simply happening *for* us and *to* us, in a most pure and honest form, throughout the week and in the times we shared together.

Comm~Unity

If we take 'comm' as a shorthand for communication and 'unity' as short for togetherness or wholeness, then what happened in our coming together in Glastonbury was, for me, the very definition of connected comm~unity.

It was a coming together, a unification and connection of dots (as Sarah would say) that we could not have dreamed up. Throughout our conversations we discovered our origin stories, how each of us had met and connected over the years. Discovering how most of us had been weaving in the digital dimension and on social media for many years, some of us for almost a decade, in ways we didn't even realise – which proved hilarious as we tried to take credit for who knew each other first and who had connected who.

Was it Kathy? Was it me? Was it Sarah? Where did we begin?

Where did we end? How did we all meet and connect to everyone in-between?

It proved to be so fascinating how each one of us connected each and another's dots. A world wide web of followers and friends. Reading each other's books and posts, coming together online through follows, comment boxes, over Zooms, Facebook groups...Seeing each other on Instagram Stories, then at conferences, workshops, talks, book launches or working together, recommending one another. The tapestry of our connected comm~unity was a wonder to behold.

This was a coming together of women in their power. Women who are friends, supporters, clients and collaborators, in different and wonderful ways. Women who left their egos at the door and stepped into their innocence as they brought out their inner child. Women who are walking their walk, talking their talk in the truth of who they are, being themselves, truly, in each moment. Letting that shine and be seen, despite navigating their insecurities and fears about coming here.

For we were gathering together shortly after the end of a very long lockdown we had experienced here in England; some of us seeing people outside of our family units or bubbles for the first time in the best part of a year. This created a magical mix, a cauldron of potent ingredients: the land, the timing, the constellation of beings for this magic to unfold.

Having been in business for almost fifteen years and attending more retreats, workshops and gatherings than I can shake a stick at, this was by far the most real version of myself that I had allowed to be seen by my contemporaries, outside of inner friendship circles. We allowed each other to simply be – to rest, to play, to heal and have fun! I usually might be more restricted or reserved in the way I show up in this environment. Not be fully all of who I am, in case I scare anyone off...And it wasn't just me that felt this. Most of us have a crazy side, a kooky, 'out there', yet at the same time introverted side that we often hide. However, here there was an unspoken permission slip which gave way for any facade or protective layer to melt away, or to blast away, with each and every Shakti fart and belly laugh that erupted.

So, aside from seeing this connected comm~unity come together, unfurl and unfold in this natural way...another nugget of gold was the way of the feminine that wanted to come through. It was a sisterhood without hierarchy and without patriarchy that took place in this space - which is rare. Usually the one(s) creating and holding the space are looked to for structure, guidance and perhaps some form of teaching or healing. What we have seen in women, especially women in business, is a mirroring of the patriarchal, capitalist, egoic ways of being, where we can often throw ourselves into doing, trying and performing within our businesses and our offerings.
Instead, this was a collaborative space. This comm~unity. This collection of unbound women, a collective of creatives, of healers and teachers, writers and leaders. The week weaved all of our healings and teachings into the space itself through our stories, our sharing, our being-ness, without the need to do, force or try. It was SO liberating. There were no timetables; instead, intentions. We stepped into this space together with a sense of PLAY. And play is what we did. Over the special days I spent with these ladies, there were sound baths, micro-dosing, arts and crafts, card readings, meditations and declarations...and that's just for starters.

To be on special and sacred land, weaving together in this way, we are not only working together as a collective - but *for* the collective.

Due to our increased use of social media and devices to communicate with one another over the past decade alongside the huge amounts of time spent apart and online, as created by the 2020 pandemic, we have become plugged in and pulled apart. It is imperative that we meet in embodied spaces with one another. Only using the tool that is social media to connect the energy threads that weave between us when we are physically apart – not for it to be the *whole* part.

I have been learning and researching over the past few years what all the screen time and time spent in digital connection is doing to our bodies and to our brains. We are out of balance. We can and should use digital communication – online comm~unity – to support and foster connections, to connect the gaps as well as the dots. However, the deeper work is the embodied work, which needs to continue, to exist and to grow again on this planet.

It is when we come together physically, not digitally, that we ground the interactions and connections that are happening all around us online, in the cloud, energetically and telepathically, too. The digital dimension is very powerful, as is the ethereal. We are yet to fully comprehend just how powerful this digital dimension could be with the building of the metaverse, where virtual and reality worlds collide with our own. Yet Gaia, Planet Earth, this universe, OUR BODIES – not the metaverse – is where the real power, the data and the energy is born from; where we are born and why we are born into these bodies at this time. I cannot stress how important it is that we gather in our embodied form, phones off, dancing and singing in a field, round a fire, holding hands, together on the land. How that very act of *being* ripples powerful and game changing repercussions throughout the ethers and dimensions when we do so.

We are in a time when the game needs to change.

I believe women and the role we play, when we come together in this way, is what will change the game. Look around us. Look at what is happening in the world. It is on metaphorical and, in some places, literal fire. We are in the midst of a changing of the guard, a spiritual war, the changing of an Age from Pisces to Aquarius. The astrology, the ancient texts and prophecies and many psychics' insights talk of this great time of change. The apocalypse, the lifting of the veil. And we only have to look around us and see what is happening to know it is not just happening by chance. This is a big one, a leap in our ascension.

Women need to come together and talk. Share stories. Support. Heal. Be. And take that back into our families and into our comm~unities.

These women that were there around me are a movement.

"*We are a fucking movement*," declared Rachel Smithbone, as we riffed over showing up from a place of love, on social media and all the spaces in between over some Peace Tea. Rachel and I, meeting for the first time in person, yet having been connected in the digital realms for some time, and energetically for lifetimes before that.

These women, you, me, we can all be part of this change. We are the change. Showing up even though we are scared. Showing up to serve each other. Sharing our talents, our gifts and our skills with each other, for the good of those around us and those connected to us. We are a movement of love, ease and sovereignty. It takes courage to be this way in the world. We have been brought up in and programmed by a world dominated by men, by the media, owned by men, by governments, run by men. Our systems have been controlled by patriarchal and capitalist corporations.

But not here. Not in this space. We are reclaiming our feminine power, our intuition and our flow. Instead, the 'rule book' was thrown out the window as we lay around, not doing anything, yet doing everything that needed to be done. There was no agenda and no agendas. There was no schedule and no big plan. There was allowing and being, within which held everything. There was trust. There was LOVE. Creating worlds and changing the world by playing, being, breathing, crying, farting and laughing.

The coming together of these women on this retreat was a beautiful reminder of how powerful it is for us to gather physically after so much time spent online. That this feminine way of working and being is better able to emerge when come together in embodied spaces. I will leave you with that inspiration and this poem, written about this moment of connection...

It is now time to gather,
to share physical space,
After meeting one another,
in a mostly digital place.

We recognise each other,
from across time and space,
We see how bright our souls shine,
from one another's face.

Scattering cyber seeds of connection,
we get ready to sow,
Embodied, circling together,
is where our roots really grow.

Our roots they weave between us,
like wise old chatty trees,
Our light pollenates each other,

like big fat bumble bees.

Connecting online to soul family,
to friends far and wide,
Makes seeing each other IRL,
A magical joyride.

About Katie Brockhurst

Sent to help navigate social media in a spiritual, ethical and healthy way that feels good for you & your nervous system...Katie is an award-winning content creator, author and experienced social media manager/consultant with over twenty years' experience. In 2020 she trained in digital wellbeing (Consciously Digital/ICF/Dip) to answer growing concerns around her own mental health and wellbeing in regard to social media, as well as that of her clients and friends. Over the last ten years she has worked with and supported well-known Hay House authors, experts and practitioners in spirituality and wellbeing to understand and manage social media. She offers one-to-one sessions, social media workshops, masterclasses and talks, as well as running the Social Media for a New Age Space on Mighty Networks, all from her home in Glastonbury, UK.

www.socialmediaforanewage.com

The Goddess Wound

by Zoë K. M. Foster

If all girls were taught
how to love each other fiercely
instead of how to compete
with each other
and hate their own bodies,
what a different and beautiful world
we would live in.

—Nikita Gill, *Fierce Fairytales*

Invited to the Party

When I first received the invitation to gather in circle with some truly amazing, inspiring and soul-aligned women in a field in Glastonbury, I balked. Truly, my gut reaction was "*Oh no, that's not for me*".

And I had to sit with that reaction for a long time to unpack all of the deep layers of hurt behind it.

On the surface level – and as someone in long-haul recovery from Topical Steroid Withdrawal – I worried I wouldn't be able to camp out in a field without really struggling to maintain the comfort of my skin, and everything that would affect it on a physical, mental, emotional and energetic plane. Sitting with this compassionately, I recognised this was just remnants of my cPTSD from the horrors of my healing crisis, and that now – in reality – this truly wasn't a big issue.

So I dug tentatively down into the subsoil a little, knowing what I'd find without having to look. Yup, there it was: I didn't believe I belonged, and it didn't feel safe to be amongst a whole group of other women – even those I loved and trusted in the online space.
And oh, once I started uncovering *that* worm-hole, there was no preventing all of the detritus coming up with it:

- When women come together, they bitch about other women behind their backs.
- Women are not safe to be yourself amongst. They will always stab you in the back. They are not genuine, loyal or trustworthy.
- Women will tear you down for your looks, your clothes, your choice of relationship, your shitty career, being too big for your boots, and every single, tiny detail of your mothering style.
- Women are literally the enemy.

This is everything society has taught me and a good deal of my personal experience.

Coming together in circles of women – even online – over the past decade has always left me feeling fraught, anxious and as if I should know how to behave – like I'm missing something crucial that all the other women know innately. As a result I've quickly felt marginalised, and even unwanted or unnecessary as a member of that particular circle. This is my default mode in any group, particularly of women.

The Wounded Feminine

I am a good girl borne from a narcissistic mother. From the earliest age I learnt to tiptoe around my mother's mercurial moods and acrimonious comments. At the age of 10 I already understood that any time she bought me something – even a new coat – I would pay for it afterwards in her emotional abuse of me. I saw right through her 'nice' phases and superficial moments of apparent connection, because I observed how she talked about others who she treated in this way: one charm-infused, sycophantic face for them; a shadow-fuelled, caustic otherness behind their backs.

As I have healed layers upon layers upon layers of this wounded-daughter syndrome, I have evolved to a much deeper and broader understanding of why this happens – and even more disturbingly, why it's far more common than you might think.

Women have been pitted against each other for centuries under the patriarchal model of society. From glossy magazines screaming about cellulite and diet pills, to TV-soap and film tropes echoing the bitchy boss, the slutty friend and the feminazi. Mired together in this toxic soup, how could we not be at war with each other?

In this way, we no longer feel safe to be in natural community with our sisters and mothers; to share our innate and ancestral wisdoms of the Earth, to honour and connect with our cycles and natural rhythms. We have been cut off from our embodied, energetic source of connection – like one of Pullman's daemons from their human counterpart. It is a manifest bastardisation of nature, the basest form of treachery to our humanity.

It's no wonder our relationships suffer as a result. We are wounded to the very core of our divine femininity.

Disarming and Disrobing Ourselves

Gathering in Glastonbury with a group of women – some I knew and loved online, and some I'd never encountered before – was profoundly heart-opening and healing for me and my deep feminine wounding. Naturally, all of my old stories rocked up around the gathering, and I let them, observing them with compassionate curiosity:

- *"I'm only coming for the day, so I won't be an integral or valued member of the group".*
- *"I'm not girly or impressive enough in my clothes, hair or make-up, and I'll be judged for that".*
- *"I'm not outgoing enough to be seen, heard and valued".*
- *"I'm not a pillar of this group anyway, so I'll be peripheral – and maybe secretly unwanted".*
- *"I have to make sure I connect with everyone and that they all like me"*
- *"I have to be on my best behaviour and show my best side".*
- *"I have to make sure I don't come across as pushy, outrageous or 'too much' of myself".*
- *"I don't really trust that everyone will honour the intention of it being a 'safe', 'show up as you are' and 'do fuck all' retreat".*
- *"I'm sure I'll feel exhausted and ostracised within about an hour of turning up".*

And so on.

What is so fascinating for me personally when I look at these statements of belief is that once upon a time, I felt thoroughly inextricable from them. The "me" I identified with was the same "me" that *knew* all of the above to be true, and this left me feeling so small that to share just one of these beliefs with another woman was off-the-charts impossible.

Thank goodness for the years of unlayering, and for finding the magical spaces where I have felt safe to share! It's only been in these spaces that I have discovered the macrame-like threads of the Goddess Wound, showing up time and time again.

During her meditations, my wonderful, magical friend Yolandi invites us to "drop our cloaks". I think that's such a perfect metaphor for our reconnection to the divine feminine, and to our deepest selves. In any relationship, when there is a genuine, mutually-embodied understanding of all of our shared and individual potential wounds and healing processes, it is so much easier to feel safe with each other. We can literally "bare all" and feel 100% OK with that.

The disarming process begins and continues with genuine connection. Sarah Lloyd set up a WhatsApp group weeks before the gathering took place, which enabled us to 'meet' and connect with everyone hoping to attend, as well as sharing whatever challenges, quibbles and insecurities that arose for us.

Setting the tone of this from the very start as a safe place to share and show up exactly as-is has been fundamental in creating a group of women who feel both deeply connected *and* held. We even had a shared playlist which any of us could add to on the theme of the retreat. Here are just some of the discussions that came up in our WhatsApp group prior to the gathering:

- Psychedelics and patriarchy
- DNA Activation
- Self-isolation woes
- Micro-dosing
- Supporting a friend's end-of-life care
- Coping with eclipse-portal challenges

- Logistics, pick-ups and food!
- Honouring friends who couldn't make the retreat

Through this gentle, compassionate disarming and disrobing process, we automatically co-created a soothing, liquid-gold healing of the divine feminine within us all.

The Little Girl Within

I didn't know until about 20 minutes into my arrival onsite that it wasn't 41-year-old Zoë showing up that day, but the little girl within me.

I got lost trying to find the place (you always know you've found a great, sacred space when the sat-nav dumps you in the middle of nowhere and says "you've arrived!") and immediately my mental tape started playing on loop again.

And then Yolandi sent me a map pin and a message to turn around, and there she was, standing in the middle of this rural road in the wilds of Somerset, like some great Goddess materialising from Mother Gaia herself. And my whole being shivered as it understood it truly belonged in this beautiful tribe of women.

Every expectation I held from previous experiences like this came up to be beautifully and lovingly dispelled. There was no flurry of introductions and names to be immediately forgotten. There was no sense of overwhelm and ensuing smallness. There was no need for forced, extroverted joviality. Instead, my memory is of a sense of peaceful, warm, welcome return – as if I'd just gone out for the day.
As I organically met each beautiful being, I felt another layer of resistance and armouring slide right off me. And as I have integrated that epic, life-changing day, three interactions in

particular impacted my whole being in ongoing waves of healing:

The Goddess Hug

Every single hug I received that day was deeply soul-nourishing, and I can honestly still feel the love shared in abundance. At the same time, it would be remiss of me not to describe the most profound hug of all which I received. Being hugged by Katherine (who I didn't yet know!) was nothing short of a healing experience. I felt absolutely seen and held, inside and out, woman-to-woman, yoni and breasts and everything in between wrapped in an all-encompassing embrace of unconditional acceptance.

Which, naturally, was terrifying and uncomfortable for me!

As a child, I was never hugged (I'm not requesting violins here, it's just a fact), and if I'm brutally honest, even lingering hugs with my husband still unnerve me. Despite the fact I hug practically everyone now, it's still a challenge for me to feel 100% received in an embrace. Part of me holds back – that part of me which doesn't feel enough in a multitude of ways.

And so, Katherine's omniscient and omnipresent, minutes-long, full-being greeting moved me through massive inner resistance to that kind of deep mind-body-soul connection. She made me feel that all of me was welcome here. *All* of me.

The Little Girl in Me Sees the Little Girl in You

At some point near the beginning of my arrival, Sarah shared that she was "honouring [her] little girl today." As soon as she said this, I felt my own inner child blow out her cheeks and sigh noisily through my whole body. The relief was visceral!

Suddenly, I realised I didn't need to show up as a gamut of adult-oriented, professional labels and attributes. My little girl could come out and play, giggle uncontrollably at fart-based humour and feel absolutely safe in similar company.

So many of us feel stuck in a role we play throughout our professional and family lives. As Sarah shared that she needed to let go of the impetus to organise and "be in charge", and to allow herself to have more fun (deep belly laughs included), it struck a deep, bass note in all of us, I think. To let ourselves simply be beyond all the labels, roles, conditioning, expectations and structures we are so used to was like being washed free of decades of baggage.

And seeing each other's little-inner-girl felt incredibly freeing and poignant. All our accumulated insecurities and adult-conditioned façades became instantly irrelevant. Suddenly, we were just a group of girls giggling with, supporting and seeing each other in full transparency and love.

Time to Drop Your Cloaks!

When women gather in absolute trust and transparency, several surprising things happen:

- We stop giving so much of a shit how we "look", both in appearance and behaviour: we dial the self-censorship and self-judgement right down! Cue sitting with open legs, showing knickers, bellies and more, cursing as much or as little as is required by the conversation, lying prone on the floor if that's what feels good, and generally honouring the call of the wild woman within – in ourselves and the other goddesses around us.

- The auto-defence mechanism instilled in us (because "women are the enemy!") relaxes significantly, if not entirely. Instead of being on the alert for a covert put-down or being shunted out of the 'cool girls' clique', we find ourselves openly giving and doing our best to receive heartfelt compliments, love and support.
- We remember and honour who we really are. This may be the most curious and counter-intuitive response of being in circle. We no longer feel compelled to fit a mould, because there's no mistrust that all of us is welcome. And every time a sister reveals a little more of her truth, it gives us the confidence to do the same. We hold the space for each other – shadows, light and everything in between.

"You haven't been here long enough; you still have a personality"

A couple of the women had just arrived. The rest of us were variously sprawled around the tent and field, fully surrendering to the exalting joys of Sarah's "smelly box", a loaded table of luscious nibbles, soul-nourishing Astral Tea, and a good deal of little-girl-fuelled banter. It was a supremely chilled, easy-going, zero-expectations kind of vibe. Kathy's voice rose in an amused, misty wave from the depths of the sofa and my first instinct (lasting approximately 0.01 nanoseconds) was to be shocked. That small part of me still on high alert felt – in that briefest instant – these women were being attacked unnecessarily for their arrival energies. But before my brain had even registered that "stress response", I was laughing and entering fully into the moment of welcoming these two wonderful ladies into an atmosphere that said, chock-full of love: *"You can relax. You don't need your façades here. You can drop all of that external-*

world bullshit. Drop your cloaks, your armouring, your safety blankets. ALL of you is welcome. Come join us!"

And with that full-body realisation and understanding, I wanted to weep ecstatic tears. Because my body suddenly felt what it would be like – what it, in fact, should be like – to exist in harmonious, supportive, loving sisterhood as an everyday norm. The suffocating, itchy cloak of hierarchical, patriarchal expectations fell to the ground. And with it went all my pre-conditioned powerlessness: my male-oriented deference and posturing for approval (attractiveness, sexiness, intellect, good-enough-ness) and female-oriented armouring and auto-defence mechanisms against competition, cliques and cut-downs.

Cloak dropped.

Regaining Sovereignty

So now I'm naked. Now we're naked (metaphorically, for the moment at least). And even though all of the questions crowd into my head at once:

- What is my default role in a group of other women?
- What role *is* there for me here?
- What role do I really *want* to play here?
- Who am I in this circle, in this space, in this moment?
- Who am I *without* all of my conditioned patriarchal fight-flight-or-freeze responses?

I also know that none of that matters – it is all a distraction from my true source and intrinsic connection to the truth of the women around me.

We may all be sisters and gather in sisterhood, and yet this does not do justice to the wound created by chronic patriarchal forces. Sisters lie to each other, steal clothes and pull hair, and yet love each other fiercely and enduringly.

No, what has been taken from us by force and chronic suppression is our inherent sovereignty – both personal and communal. Within myself I am now able to see with extrasensory lucidity the effects of my ancestral conditioning reaching back millennia. I see my bottomless lack of self-worth masquerading as buoyant survivalism. I see my automatic default with women is to armour up in defence and with men, it is a fawning deference. And I see that this is how we've been taught to serve a humanity ruled and regulated by men, who are themselves deeply wounded.

We have willingly renounced our sovereignty as a means to survive.

But now, gathering in circle and dropping our cloaks in unison, we are rising again. Layer by layer, we shed our personal and collective trauma *together*. And in doing so we gently, lovingly remind each other of our glittering, indomitable, expansive divinity.

We are human, yes – but we are also goddesses. Not just sisters supporting each other through the mire: *goddesses*. And the Goddess Wound runs so deep that our first instinct is to scoff, to covertly or overtly tear down any sister claiming her own crown precisely because *we fear our own*.

If we claim our divine feminine sovereignty then we can no longer hide in victimhood, survivalism and eternal deference to the wounded masculine systems and structures which govern our world and determine our current reality.

We must be vulnerable in our co-operation.

We must consciously heal the incalculable layers of our wounded feminine.

We must be willing to meet each other, heart-to-heart and womb-to-womb.

We must commit to seeing and truly honouring the little girl within each of us.

We must disarm, disrobe and drop the heavy cloak of patriarchal rule.

And we must choose to rise and radiate together.

About Zoë K.M. Foster

Exploring our Cosmic Humanity through sacred, embodied expression

Zoë K. M. Foster is on a quest to uncover and rebirth the deep soul of our world. As an artist and writer, she fully embodies this energetic intention to create immersive, profoundly sensual and multi-sensory experiences through her large-scale abstract art, poetry, meditations and reflections.

She is also the creator of SacredExpression™ Yoga: a playful, whole-body experience involving life-size paper, coloured pastels, sacred geometry and divine feminine immersion to help you tap into your deepest soul messages and integrate them fully into your conscious, everyday evolution!

Zoë's background in cognitive psychology, linguistics, design and yoga allow her to play with – and hold sacred space for – the many tensions between what we expect, and what actually *most* needs to be expressed – both personally and collectively.

This is where tantra, embodiment work and cosmic spirituality step in to free us from the shackles of Greek thinking, and what we find there is an unseen space beyond polarities: an infinite spectrum of possibility.

Through her YouTube show, 'Core Truths', Zoë hosts intimate conversations with soul-driven changemakers all playing their part in birthing the new world. She digs down right to the core light of who we are and what motivates, inspires and drives us as individuals, as humanity and even as an integral player within the universe itself...

You can find Zoë and all of her current offerings at zoekmfoster.com and on social media **@zoekmfoster**.

Immiscible Soul – A Tale Of Overcoming Social Anxiety Through Self-Love

by Rachel Smithbone

I am the vehicle for what needs to be said. The themes are personal and also universal. I offer myself to this piece of wisdom.

I think when I consider my chapter, a lot comes up. I wanted to be a part of this collaborative body of work, to add my voice to the piece because (I am good enough, I am worthy, I stand amongst and alongside my friends and colleagues) when I was on retreat with them, I felt a deep stirring, a calling.

I could sense that some kind of movement was being born and every ragged, torn fibre of hope within me wants to be part of that.

I grew up loving and studying literature and to imagine myself as part of a movement was like living in a Disney film – except that my heroines saved their own asses whilst wielding pens and self-awareness! Our weapons are our faith, our hope, our soul work and our words.

Through the power of intention and defiance, social media has brought us together, in an age where social media is tearing folks apart. We are the rebels. We are the wayfinders. We are the women rising up and saying, *"enough of this shit*". Writing was a common theme within our group (I am enough, I deserve to be here, my fear is not as overbearing as my acceptance is transformative); we all use writing in some respect within our work and our beings.

My whole life I dreamed of having the identity of 'writer'; being able to call myself a 'writer' and all of the magic that was tied with that one simple idea. The knowing that I sit outside of society and my perspective and wisdom helps others to understand it; the knowing that my words will elicit deep feelings and hope within others. There is a feeling of being enough when I claim the title of writer.

I studied writing at university, but all it did was convince me that I wasn't good enough to claim that for myself. Not so any longer. I claimed it and here I am: a writer, in a movement.

Writing this chapter, meeting with my friends and colleagues after the retreat to discuss the ripples that have echoed through our lives since we came together in person in Glastonbury after a global pandemic, the themes that are emerging individually and within us as a collective are thought-provoking and inspiring. Perhaps they will spark something in your heart and mind, perhaps they will make you look at things a little differently, perhaps they will make you send out the siren call for your own sisterhood.

I want to share with you my personal journey, the deep significance that meeting these women in person had for me that day. I am a powerful being, a Conscious Entrepreneur who spends her time supporting women to love themselves and BE themselves. This journey is a part of me walking my talk. This piece is a deepening of that same process.

Excited? Me too! Here we go.

Pre-Retreat Perceptions

I've always been an outlier, a fact that has been very obvious and kind of painful my whole life. I am blessed to have amazing friends, friends that love me unequivocally and unconditionally for who I am. We share enough commonality that we feel safe to be ourselves. I have spent a lot of my life loving people who accept me for who I am, but not surrounded by people that particularly share my passions for spirituality and business.

There is something magical in coming together with women who share your beliefs and aspirations, who get the things that you believe rather than simply accepting them. The feeling of being in a clan of like-minded souls was magical, exhilarating and soul soothing.
Immiscible.

(You are safe, dear one. You are. You are not broken. You are not too much. You are not too little. You are enough.)

You wouldn't know it to look at me but I have always struggled with debilitating social anxiety, the kind that drives you to drink too much, to cancel plans, to shy away from the world and new experiences.

When the incredible Sarah Lloyd said that she was running a retreat and invited me, a cascade of swirling oily and watery emotions spiralled through my being. The immiscible combination left me in a familiar state of inner conflict: on the one hand desperately wanting to go and on the other hand, terrified at the thought of intimate time in an established group of women.

It's nothing new. It is an old and very well-worn garment. A garment that has dug deeply into me; too tight, too restrictive, painfully uncomfortable. A garment that I feared may well be glued to the very fabric of my being.

I desperately wanted to go for two compelling reasons. Firstly, I wanted to be part of something magical: a group of grounded, awakened entrepreneurs all doing incredible work in the world. I belonged in that group and wanted to claim my place on that stage. I wanted to be part of it, part of SOMETHING.

Secondly, I believed that my story of social anxiety was a tale that had finally reached a conclusion in my life. Quite simply, I wasn't that person anymore and attending this retreat would be evidence to support my belief. I have done so much inner work, felt so deeply empowered and committed to self-love. It was time to put my money where my mouth was.

The stakes were high.

I felt truly powerful. Powerful from my inner core. I felt that going on retreat with these women would be proof that the work that I had done was real. Proof that I have truly learned to love who I am.

In some way, I knew that I would be able to cope with the deep anxiety that had always accompanied me around social gatherings like this.

So, I decided to go.

In the months leading up to the retreat, the anxiety did surface in geyser spurts, but they passed as quickly as they came and my resolve to go didn't falter.

I decided to go for one night, to dip my toe in the water rather than belly flop straight in.

June 2021: Banbury Meadow, Glastonbury – Retreat Riffs

I felt like I was a part of something powerful forming and emerging. I felt like one of the gang. I felt seen and heard. I felt so much love and compassion (*are they judging me, taking the piss out of me, humouring me*? Rejection. A fear of being rejected.) I wanted to hear every conversation. I loved that everyone shared my interests!

It felt so good to be a part of something, to be seen, to be an equal with these incredible women. Women of such a powerful and loving vibration. Women coming together to lift, to inspire, to laugh and love with one another.

I am learning to feel safe and these women felt like a safe space to do that in. I didn't have to moderate or translate to be understood. They got it. Each and every one of them. They understand about self-development and growth, they understand about holding space for another, about sovereignty and self-responsibility.

Imagine if I had let my own lingering crumbs of self-doubt and anxiety stop me going. It was a space of healing and I wish that I could have it all over again and meet myself at an even deeper level.

During the retreat, I said that I'd never been able to fully be myself in a group of women. That's true, but it only ever came from me, not from the other women. It came from being uncomfortable in who I was. Not feeling loveable.

Concerned that if I let myself 'out' I would be too much or not enough. Too loud, taking up too much space and at the same time not funny or entertaining enough – boring.

BORING.

That lands. It lands like someone else's soggy old flannel on my face.

It is unignorable and kinda gross.

I have been very scared to be 'boring'. Why? I judge others as 'boring' and I judge others for being 'hard work' – souls that are not at peace with themselves and are awkward – I feel it with so much pain and I internalise that pain and discomfort and I want to RUN from it. It is a horrible mirror to how I have felt and how I have tried to hide.

Except that I am not that person anymore.

I was very pleased to only be going for a day to the retreat and very pleased to be able to go to my own room and get to sleep when I wanted to. Not being able to escape.

I was pleased to have people there that I knew. It made it feel safer.

Social situations are exhausting. They make me so tired and yet I love getting to know people. I love hearing their stories.

There is something going on inside me that is trying really hard and that gets tiring very quickly! I give so much energy when I am chatting to people.

I also try to say the right thing. I find it really hard when I have nothing to say! I try to manufacture things. (I can't be the only one that feels this way, can I?)

I used to feel crippling anxiety – the fear of not being able to connect with someone and for the conversation not to flow and then getting trapped with them and not knowing how to escape that situation. The fear of getting really tired and having nowhere to escape to. Twice I have chosen the word 'escape' and it's a very interesting choice of words, isn't it? I am not trapped in those situations and yet I feel trapped. I feel like I can't get away. I am so concerned about what other people think of me. It trumps what I need and feel in that moment.

"I don't know how to talk to people!" That's what just popped into my head when I was imagining a retreat! I don't know how to talk to people. I don't know how to laugh and joke and mess about and have fun. Everyone seemed so funny and carefree when they were growing up and I don't know how to do that. Even on the calls discussing writing this piece, Sarah was saying how she just wants to keep it FUN, just like the retreat was, but I don't know how to do that! I LOVE fun, but I am also a deeply serious and sensitive person and that side of me gets forced to the shadows.

Writing this piece is deeply cathartic because I have allowed myself space to just be me. For the piece to be boring and heavy and for that to be OK.

My story of social anxiety is a story of not loving myself as I am. Believing, falsely, that I am a boring person; that my own needs in social situations aren't important, that if I allow myself to be fully me then I won't be likeable.

I have been terrified of upsetting or offending people, of getting it wrong, of being too much or too little. Perhaps I just didn't like myself very much: I certainly wasn't at all confident in who I was.

"It's not all about you"

I so wanted to be like my friends who are confident and don't give a shit. They're just loud and brash and funny and themselves and people can love them or not, it doesn't matter.

Longing. I am feeling a deep longing to be back in the proximity of the gang. The women that have come together in that space. The retreat was an expansion for me but I held tightly to the edges of the container, allowed myself to only stretch little by little for fear that I may break.

The Immediate Aftermath

In the aftermath of this tentative expansion, I have felt so magnificent that the deep longing has arisen inside of me. Something was alchemised and the social anxiety that I have been reluctantly embalmed within for so much of my life has completely dissolved.

I feel set free.

Revived.

The other day, I was at a social gathering of extended family on my husband's side and as we gathered with the unsettling and separative stench that the Covid world leaves in the air, I found myself in a very familiar internal experience. My body clenched. I became heavy and separate inside. I didn't want to be there and I didn't want to interact with anyone.

Previously, this feeling would have left me spiralling into a vortex of shame and self-flagellation: "*What is wrong with you? These people are your family. Why can't you just be NORMAL and socialise like NORMAL people? Why do you ALWAYS do this? Why can't you get past this? It's pathetic, it's just a normal part of life...*" and on and on.

But this time it played out very differently. The sensations arose but no dialogue came with it. I noticed how I felt. I was curious and compassionate and I took myself quietly away to allow the sensations to move through my body. Without shame, without inner flagellation, without resistance, they simply passed, clouds on a breezy summer's day.

It was a marvellous thing to experience.

It leaves me longing again to experience the intimacy of these magical women from the retreat. The promise of who I can be, who I am meant to be. The promise of a world of experience opening up before me and within me.

All the things that I have said no to in my life because of the unpleasantness, discomfort and downright anguish of being in community.

August 2021: Two Months On

It's been almost exactly two months since we were on retreat together. We have been communicating almost daily in the WhatsApp group and it feels really good to be a part of that group. I think if I am honest, I would love to go back and have it all over again and sit with all the emotions that could come up. To process them, to move through them, to be with the discomfort and to move through it. I would LOVE to be back on retreat and able to be with these women and to chat and talk to them, each of them, to get to know them even more, to dare to be vulnerable and to risk getting it wrong and also to know that it was a deeply safe space to get it wrong. That we are all doing our own inner work – that we all know how to hold space for each other. As I read this, I realise that I long for them as a playground to trigger me, trigger the unresolved boils of not-enoughness to blister and pop so that I can gently scrape them clean and allow the healing to take hold. This is the power of true sisterhood.

September 2021: Rich Reflections & Seismic Echoes

It's now been three months since we were on retreat and the seismic echoes continue to make their presence felt. Recently, some of us met up again at a gorgeous harbourside hotel in Southampton, amongst yachts and cocktails. I was talking to one of the Goddesses about my feelings of social anxiety and how the retreat had helped me to know that I have transmuted them. She asked me: *"Did you feel anxious about coming here today?"*

The question floored me.

I had not even given it a second thought. I had instigated it. I had been so desperate to see these women again.

Anxious, no, not even for a milli-moment. The wound had gently healed and not even scar tissue remained. I get to be me. I get to love myself in my messy, loud, quiet and chaotic self. I have a group of people around me who get it. Who get me.

I wanted to contribute to this body of work to share my experience of overcoming social anxiety, of reclaiming a part of myself that had not felt good enough or safe to BE. I also wanted to be a part of something. I feel like there is a big shift happening at a collective level within the Western world. I have always felt that things were deeply out of alignment, but not known what to do with that feeling – beyond supporting people to love themselves and to come home to the spiritual truth of who and what they are.

It can feel deeply lonely when you are an outlier, when you long for things to be different. When this group of women met and there was a tangible vibration of change in our combined energy field, it made me feel hope. Hope that I am not alone in this quest. Hope that there are more gifted, talented souls working every day to do what is in their hearts to do. Hope that the world can indeed change to live in greater harmony and love.

I wanted to be a part of this because I don't want to do this work alone anymore. I want to be held, supported and loved in community. We are small pockets of souls doing the foundational work and it can feel terribly hopeless at times when faced with a humanity that seems hell bent on destroying itself.

But...

Just like in our distant tribal past, we are stronger when we are together. We are more productive when we are together. We can effect change when we are together.

My journey was a personal one; it took a lot of courage and inner work to get to this place. Now that I am here, I know that the sisterhood supports me to expand further into who I AM and that society needs me to do so. I know that what once felt lonely and divided now feels unified and fierce. I know that I am enough. That my contribution is enough. That the sum of our parts is amplified, magnificent versions of ourselves. The immiscible parts of oil and water have alchemised into something clear and conductive, a fluid to amplify the whispers of change.

About Rachel Smithbone

Rachel Smithbone, aka the High Priestess of Sacred Self-Love and Spiritual Badassery, is best known for her work supporting soulful beings to love themselves fully and unconditionally. Rachel is passionate about the Universe and as a Priestess works to support others to create deep and loving relationships with the Divine. Rachel has a unique gift for creating deeply transformational energetic experiences. As a master space holder, Rachel combines her diverse and original skillset as a qualified yoga teacher, gong therapist, intuitive energetic channel and natural shaman to support her mission to elevate the consciousness of humanity through unified and devotional living with the Divine. When she's not cavorting around her ancestral farm on the Exmoor National Park or playing in the ancient woodland with her hubby and two feral children, you can find Rachel offering bespoke 1-2-1 transformational coaching packages, sacred sound ceremonies and her online membership The Self-Love Sanctuary. Find out more and work with Rachel by visiting **www.rachelsmithbone.co.uk**

The Retreat Is Just The Beginning

by Michelle Maslin-Taylor

I remember how I felt when I first read *The Universe Has Your Back* by Gabby Bernstein, followed by *Light Is the New Black* by Rebecca Campbell. These books changed my life; I suddenly felt less alone and I realised for the first time that the way I felt was not unique, there were other women just like me who were spiritual, not religious. Suddenly, my deep sense of knowing and connection made sense. Those books unravelled my stories and learned rules around religion and spirituality; I felt like I could breathe and expand for the first time. Suddenly, my spirituality was unbound. How funny and not at all a coincidence (thank you, universe) that I've ended up here, with a group of women equally unbound in their spirituality, sharing their souls with The Unbound Press. I do love a little bit of serendipity and synchronicity.

Back to these books and the women inside them. These women I could relate to started off on paper, but what I longed for was to find them in real life, to attract in a tribe where I wouldn't feel so weird, where I could talk about energy and the universe and my intuition and have that received and understood. I needed sisterhood.

You see, growing up I felt lonely a lot. I have a sister, but our connection is not a typical sister one, if there is such a thing. Being autistic with very limited speech, socialising, gossiping and chatting for hours is not her thing. She is sensitive, sweet and kind but definitely would not have wanted to hear all my dramas – those were saved for the poor pet rabbit in the garden!

I was (and am) sensitive, intuitive and naturally introverted and wore (and wear) my heart on my sleeve. At school I found other girls to be cruel, critical and inauthentic. As an adult in the workplace, often more of the same. I learned that women are often not supportive of other women. Maybe that's why I stayed in a male-dominated industry for so long, working as a web developer for nearly two decades. Of course, I also met some wonderful women, but I was wary – that heart on my sleeve was ripped right off and stamped on.

These wounds stayed with me, as all unhealed wounds do. In yoga we think of samskaras, which are habits formed from imprints of actions and reactions. I think of them like grooves or rivers that get deeper and harder to escape each time you repeat the same pattern of thought or behaviour. The deeper they engrain, the harder to claw your way back out. Mine brought tendencies towards self-doubting, staying small and trying to be unnoticed at all costs.

You may be wondering if you've strayed into the wrong book right now. *What has this got to do with a women's retreat, Michelle*?

Well, I'll let you into a little secret. Even though I am a yoga teacher, I haven't actually been on a retreat myself before as a participant. Between my introverted nature, three young children and a busy schedule, it's just something I haven't had time for. No, let's be honest here – it's something I haven't prioritised or made happen. I've stayed in my comfort zone and in learned patterns, shied away and felt shackled by responsibility whilst secretly feeling relief that I didn't have to face the inevitable comparison of being in a space of women without the distraction of being the one to organise, hold space and facilitate healing. I know I'm good at that, it comes naturally. Socialising, well, that's a bit scary!

Phew. That's a big confession. And here comes another in the form of the first of my lessons learned on retreat because that's what I really want to share with you. I love a lesson and retreats – well, they serve up a heap of them if you are open to receiving.

Lesson #1: You don't always go home feeling all love, light and magical

Returning from the retreat, I fell on the bed and cried. I cried on and off for days. Not tears of joy, relief and gratitude, but big, salty, wet tears of complete unworthiness, of not-enoughness, of despair that the path I've chosen for my life is not for me, of failure.
Who were these bullies that made me feel such a way?

That's the thing, there were no bullies, no unkind words, no gossiping, whispering or funny looks. These women I had just returned from spending time with were open, kind, authentic and welcoming. This feeling was all me: all my insecurities bubbling to the surface, not being able to stop my compulsion to compare myself to these glorious goddesses.

It's like all things, that growth edge. You have to be willing to face the illusion and grieve its loss to be able to clearly see the truth. It's hard. Healing is hard. Community is sometimes hard. Letting go is hard. Rebirth is hard but the more you resist it, the more it will come knocking.

Taking that pain and poking the wound, allowing myself to feel it and see where it came from was healing and painful at the same time, for these wonderful women accepted me as

I am and if people as wonderful as them can love me in my imperfection then I certainly can find a way to too.

But, be warned: you may not come back from retreat all glowy and serene, you may be a midst-of-healing hot mess. And that's okay.

On to the next reminder that the retreat gifted me.

Lesson #2: Serendipity and synchronicity are all around

Serendipity. This is my favourite word of all time, I've already used it once in this chapter. If you've ever seen the movie of the same name, you'll recognise the line: "*it's such a nice sound for what it means: a fortunate accident...Except I don't really believe in accidents. I think fate's behind everything*".

This resonates deeply with me and let me tell you a little bit about the serendipitous events that led me to this particular group and this particular retreat because when you piece together all the random meetings and connect all the dots, the interweaving of connections and crossed paths is truly magical. I can't believe that these were all chance, but more of a journey of paths that had to meet.

Let's start with Sarah. Magical Sarah. We first met years ago at a local wellbeing event, with our little fold-up tables on other ends of the community centre – my first event since qualifying as a yoga teacher and her first event offering reiki and card readings. It was suggested I talk to her about finding other events and I nervously shuffled over to her table. She was back-to-back booked so we just exchanged details and didn't meet up again until months later, but the connection was made and has grown into a beautiful friendship. We both felt the call to connect again even though we only exchanged a few words when we met. It was a bit of a magical blind date!

Nicola, the wonderful founder of The Unbound Press, was like an Instagram celebrity to me. I had followed for a little while, won her book through an Instagram competition and even recommended her to a friend looking to publish her book (which, of course, she is, by the way). Somehow, we ended up on this retreat together. As if by chance? As if.

Many of the other ladies I knew of through the power of social media too; it was almost like a celebrity dinner for me, being gathered in a field together.

To be honest, I was completely intimidated by them. These women were confident and successful in my eyes, spiritual badass business owners. Where I should fit (in theory), but I still felt like an outsider. Fate brought us all together at exactly this moment, in this place, with all our shared connections. The universe does not make mistakes.

Serendipity and synchronicity – love notes from the universe.

Talking of the connections made...

Lesson #3: True connection can be instant or a slow burner

Wisdom from the connections I made came in the weeks and months following the retreat. We expect to go away for a night or a week and come back changed, refreshed and healed but the truth is far messier and more complicated than that. Healing is a little like grief, it comes in waves and hits you unexpectedly in random moments and sometimes the people to hold you through that process are close to strangers, women you've only met for a couple of days but somehow KNOW you.

These women are now my go-to when anything "woo woo"

pops up, when my faith in myself waivers, when I need to rant, when I want to pack it all in, or when I have a flash of inspiration and need to share...they've got me. And your retreat tribe will have you too.

Now that's sisterhood.

And one of those sisters, well, she taught me how to make friends with strangers! Cue the next lesson.

Lesson #4: How to make friends online (courtesy of Kathy Fucking Bell)

I don't make friends easily. Actually, that's an over-simplification – maybe it's just that it has to be the right people, that they have to be patient for me to warm up and to not take my introverted and shy nature as standoffishness.

I've been told that I can be intense. I make a lot of eye contact and I don't do small talk. I want to look into your eyes and speak to your soul. I'm definitely not for everyone. I'm open and vulnerable and it makes a lot of people uncomfortable. I've come to realise that it's not my responsibility to make everyone comfortable, it's my responsibility to be me.

In the spiritual space it can be tricky to find your tribe. Despite what you may think, not all yoga teachers think the same, not all spiritual people think the same and my experience is that there can be a lot of competition and judgement. It's definitely not all light out there, sometimes more yogi-eat-yogi. You're not spiritual enough or yogi enough, or you're too much. You're always not enough **and** too much, it depends on who you ask. Finding the people for whom you are just right is the sweet spot.

It took me a decade living in Surrey to make a handful of

wonderful friends, completely on board with me as I am. At the time of writing this I have recently moved counties and despite considering myself a bit of a loner, the truth is I still get lonely: I crave connection, but just not any old connection.

Something Kathy said on retreat stuck with me, speaking about how she reaches out to people online who she feels connection with, kinda a "hey, do you want to be my friend?" message. My mind was blown. Could I be that brave to ever do that?

Let me tell you wonderful souls that I was that brave and you can be too. I met a lady selling crystals (of course) at a school fair and exchanged details after chatting about all things woo and I reached out online and asked if she would like to go for a walk one day. It was scary AF for me: *What if she thinks I'm weird? What if she ghosts me? What if she says no?* My inner child was braced for rejection but instead she found connection.

My first friend made at my new home, all thanks to a little nugget of wisdom learned on retreat.

Thank you, Kathy, for teaching me how to make friends!

Lesson #5: Your gifts are reflected back to you

At the time of this particular retreat my business, like so many others, had been thrown the Covid curveball. I was yoga teaching just once a week online and hadn't practiced reiki on anyone other than myself for over a year, having chosen not to take on any distant healing with a crazy busy household that was distinctly lacking in any sacred (and quiet) space. Whilst retreating I was asked if I would give some reiki healing to my wonderful goddess of a coach, Rosie. Of course, I jumped at the chance, even though I was secretly filled with fear that maybe I'd lost my mojo by now. That moment was such a gift, a reminder of my own gifts as I felt energy start to flow and received a message to pass on. After so much forced time off from my healing work I wonder if I would have continued without that moment, whether the lost confidence that time had brought would have just extended into a permanent healing hiatus.

Would reiki have become my little secret, reserved just for my bedtime self-healing routine?

What a shame that would have been, as reiki was such an essential for me in getting through the dreaded "C" season. That moment reminded me of how important it was for me to continue to share it, feeling completely in flow, aligned and tuned in. Since then it has been crystal clear that it is the core of my work in this world, my dharma to infuse it in to all that I do.

Now the next lesson might already be clear since most of what I've shared has been post-retreat but finally...

Lesson #5: What happens on retreat doesn't stay on retreat

Okay, that is a little misleading, I don't mean that everyone goes away and gossips and spills the private beans. Rather, the healing that starts on retreat – the conversations, the connections, the inner work, the triggers – they all come with you and expand and evolve. The retreat is a catalyst for healing that continues long after you return to using regular toilets and private showers.

Phew, that's a lot of healing post-retreat and we all know that healing can be rough. Was it worth it? Absofuckinlutely. The retreat was just the start, now we have community.

Community isn't all niceties, yoga classes and dinners together – it's raw, honest and real. Having a group hold space for you to let out your frustrations without trying to fix them, simply to witness them.

If something has been holding you back from retreating, I encourage you to take a leap. If there is one that you feel called to, a teacher you are drawn to, see where it leads you. How does it make you feel? (Note: There's a difference between excited but nervous and just plain nervous). If it feels like a yes, it's a yes – get packing!

But be warned, the retreat is just the beginning...

Love & light,

Michelle.

About Michelle Maslin-Taylor

Michelle is a certified yoga teacher, Reiki Master and coach. She harnesses the power of ancient practices and yoga psychology for emotional balance and healing, offering reiki-infused yoga and coaching to women ready to connect to become their own guru.

Having overcome depression, negative body image and low self-esteem with the power of yoga and personal development, she is dedicated to empowering women worldwide to stop outsourcing their health and happiness and take control of their mental and physical wellness.

She is passionate about creating health and happiness in a fully holistic way, honouring the intrinsic link between our energy body and the physical, sharing the benefits of yoga, reiki and meditation as a part of a holistic toolbox to begin facilitating our own healing.

Download free workbooks and meditations and connect with Michelle at **www.michellemaslintaylor.com**

Should I Stay Or Should I Go?

by Iona Russell

I opened my heart to death and she passed through, leaving within me a vastness that echoed soundlessly: *"...and now what?"* The space that unexpectedly enveloped me was overwhelming and unfamiliar yet recognisable as I felt lost, again.

My divine Shakti sisters were all preparing to meet in Glastonbury, and I was stood in an empty room that had been home to my friend only days ago. Her dying had kept me distracted for the last four weeks as we created the sacred space for her to transition with dignity, grace and belly laughs.

Within this time, I was able to reflect on that which wasn't important, wasn't necessary, the shoulds, the hustle, the personal and societal expectations of being a woman, a mum, an entrepreneur, a coach...and I began let go. I realised I'd been over-doing, over-committing, over-subscribing and trying to be in control by being busy, being, busy. (Let's not go down the path of discussing being busy is a trauma response, that's a story for another time.)

And yet as I stood there in silence, I was already making a list of all the things to do 'next' so that I could make the nine-hour drive to Glastonbury, because this was going to be fun with a capital F-U-N. BUT I'd still need to 'deal' with sorting this room, get rid of the hospital bed, the oxygen tanks, repaint it and put all my stuff back in it to reclaim my sitting room upon my return.

This retreat 'would' or 'could' be impactful for my business, deepen connections, birth new collaborations and ideas. This was the break of routine I was looking for, but my routine had stopped and it was now vastly empty. I knew being around women, other soul-led, heart inspired SiSTARS would feed my soul and nourish my whole being.

But I also had a tug of war going on between feeling the need to withdraw to go within and sit in the emptiness, and a very loud bellowing dominatrix of FOMO and she was angry: "*YOU COMMITTED, YOU SAID YOU'D BE THERE, AND WHAT IF YOU MISS OUT ON AMAZING BUSINESS OPPORTUNITIES?*"

I chose to listen to the quiet inner voice that was whispering from the hollows of my heart. I chose to pause, rest and reset. I chose to stay home.

In this space I got to BE in the presence of what was enveloping me and allowed the space to expand with the unravelling and revealing of the magic of the deep connection to something bigger than me. To understand that each life is a gift, so precious and unique. You might wonder, *but surely, Iona, you already know that*? Yes, but I got to embody it with a deeper knowing. Having the gift of witnessing my friend's beautiful human life end and transition is something I will treasure for eternity.

So often as women in business we can get caught up in the merry-go-round of the circus around us and turn into a performing lioness, and in this process we lose sight of who we are and our own inner magic and the divine essence of the impact we are here to have on the world. For I truly believe each and every one of us is here to make a difference, to create from our heart and live our soul's purpose.

In my friend's passing, her death, her transition taught me that our philosophical standpoints are personal but it's our value system that links us. It's funny, but people got so weirded out in my talking about death with such ease. I see her 'death' as beautiful and as part of the cycle of the seasons, for we each return to the cosmos and the oneness which we only lose sight of in our human form.

What is everyone afraid of? What are you afraid of? Are you running away from life or are you running away from death? Are you embracing your life? Are you living each day as a gift to be celebrated?

My friend wasn't religious or spiritual by any stretch of the imagination. She and her husband were very practical in their approach. We all knew why she was at my house and that death was imminent, no and, ifs or buts. This was her ending and by heck was she choosing to do it her way.

I witnessed such love between two life-long partners as her human body started to shut down and fail her. We spent much time talking and laughing when she was able. In these conversations we uncovered our similarities in our approach to life, and our core values on making a difference and having an impact. Both her and her partner loved their work, their careers that they had only just retired from. They were driven by a purpose greater than themselves to make the world a better place, to help those less fortunate and to help one person at a time in their chosen careers. They both did this tenfold.

The one thing they were both grateful for is that they didn't wait for 'one day' to travel to explore the world and go on adventures. You might have driven past them cycling around

Europe on a bicycle made for two. You might have seen them canoeing along the river and stopping for a picnic. You might have walked past them hiking in the mountains carrying all their belongings, a million miles away from civilisation. They didn't wait for 'one day', they embraced living today.

In choosing to stay home and not attend the gathering, I was dancing between a smorgasbord of contradictory feelings, wondering if by not going I was not living in the moment, shrugging off building connections and adventures that would serve my wellbeing and my business; maybe I wasn't embracing today.

I shouldn't have worried. I felt so energetically connected to the gathering as they continued to share in the WhatsApp chat, getting lost, finding each other, photos of moments, belly laughs and cosmic cuddles. I felt them on a deep level in the undercurrents of the pause I had created for myself.

This was my contribution. The Pause Effect.

Giving us all permission, a gentle reminder that we are all connected no matter where we are. First we get to honour our divine selves, and then we get to show up for each other from this place of fully fucking unbound magic of feminine fabulousness: from this energetic stance, we are unstoppable.

In the pause I felt my friend's presence, her beauty, her light within the room she transitioned from. I tuned into my SiSTARS in Glastonbury and I cleansed my home and I painted her room. I claimed back my space and wished her well on her journey.

My journey continues with wondering, curiosity and celebration. Knowing we are all connected and energy doesn't die; energy is everything and we are all part of the everything, the oneness.

The magic is that your presence can be felt no matter where you are, if you choose to connect.

I choose joy, and I choose to breathe in the beauty of living and dying as reflected in human life, in our businesses, in our loves, in our relationships in the seasons of our dreams and connections. To each unfolding, new beginning and new ending, everything is timeless and seamless.

I invite you to look at what you are choosing to do and not do and explore why.

Your business is a reflection of you. If you aren't fully embodied into your soulful Being, you can't show up and have the impact you wish to have. If you are running around doing all the 'shoulds, musts and need-tos', ignoring your inner wisdom on what is right for you in that moment, you will continue to feel like you are hustling and out of alignment.

In letting go and not going, I was actually more present with them and more present with me.

About Iona Russell

Iona Russell is a Master Positive Psychology Coach, Clinical Hypnotherapist, speaker, author and radio host. She works with creatives, visionaries and entrepreneurs to transform their lives and businesses, bridging the gap between evidence based Positive Psychology and New Age Wisdom in aligning mind, body and soul for their self-empowered personal freedom, fulfilment and prosperity, with a sense of personal freedom that fuels the elation and excitement for their future.

Iona does this through:

- Deep energy work
- Positive Psychology
- Past Life Regression
- Unconscious beliefs
- Quantum mindset shifts
- Clinical Hypnotherapy
- Inner child work
- NLP (Neuro-Linguistic Programming)
- Quantum Dynamic Healing

You can find out more about Iona and her work here:
www.ionarussell.com

What's Next?

We hope you've enjoyed journeying with us through *Shakti Farts & Belly Laughs*, magical one.

If you'd like to stay in touch and find out more about gatherings we're hosting in the future, both online and in person, then head to theunboundpress.com/shakti-farts and sign-up to receive updates.

Printed in Great Britain
by Amazon

86369400R00071